MODERN BAROQUE
INTERIORS

daab

Introduction

INTRODUCTION

Artistic movements have oscillated like a pendulum between opposite trends for centuries. In some periods purity and simplicity of form were the key elements, whereas in others the leitmotif was complexity and voluptuousness, such as the Baroque styles, which reigned in Europe during the 17th and the first half of the 18th century. The Catholic Church's necessity to move and excite the people and the will of the monarchies to express their triumphant power were the principal factors, along with others which led to the birth of this style characterised by its ostentatious and over elaborate shapes.

In recent years the World of Decoration has recreated this movement splendidly with the new baroque style, based on a revamp of its characteristics, which is already being seen on the catwalks. The profusion of curved forms, the excessive use of materials and color and the mysteriousness of light and shadows have been reinterpreted in many kinds of interiors. Sometimes, the architectural structure itself is the main reason why structures like the palaces and period buildings have been carefully restored to regain their charming essence. However in other buildings it is the stark contrast between the simplicity and minimalism of the structure and this radiant new baroque decoration which triumphs. The most remarkable achievements are without any doubt the furniture – often inspired by the style of Louis XV – the decorative objects such as majestic chandeliers, candle holders, engraved mirrors and glassware. The glitter and colors such as gold, silver, burgundy and black portray the essence of baroque in this new expression of its sophisticated and luxurious nature. It is also worth remembering that the evolution of the production methods, as well as the increase in the use and quality of materials such as plastic or resin have favoured the return of the curve, in such a way that this key element of the baroque style has resurfaced as its most representative symbol.

Die künstlerischen Bewegungen sind im Laufe der Jahrhunderte zwischen entgegengesetzten Strömungen hin- und hergependelt. Einige Epochen zeichneten sich durch die Reinheit und Einfachheit der Formen aus, während andere die Vielschichtigkeit und Üppigkeit bevorzugten. So war es auch im Barockstil der Fall, der Europa während des 17. und in der ersten Hälfte des 18. Jhs. beherrschte. waren Zwei Faktoren führten zu der Entstehung dieses Stils, der von überladenen und prunkvollen Formen gekennzeichnet ist: die Notwendigkeit, das Volk zu bewegen und zu begeistern, der sich die katholische Kirche angesichts der Bedrohung durch den Protestantismus ausgesetzt sah, und der Wille der absoluten Monarchien, ihre Macht auf repräsentative Weise zu demonstrieren.

Während der letzten Jahre haben Kreative auf der ganzen Welt diese Bewegung im Stil des Neobarock wiederentdeckt, fortgeführt und ihre dekorativen Elemente auf wundervolle Weise variiert. Dieser Trend begann auf den Laufstegen der Welt. Ein Überfluss an gebogenen Formen, ein großzügiger Einsatz von Materialien und Farben sowie das geheimnisvolle Spiel mit hellen und dunklen Effekten wurde in allen möglichen Räumen aufgegriffen. Manchmal spielt die architektonische Struktur selbst die Hauptrolle, so in den Palästen und Gebäuden aus der Epoche des Barock, die mit großer Sorgfalt restauriert wurden, um die berauschende Essenz dieses Stils zu erhalten. In anderen Gebäuden wiederum triumphiert der Gegensatz zwischen der Einfachheit und dem Minimalismus der Struktur und einer prunkvollen, neobarocken Dekoration. Die auffallendsten Elemente sind ohne Zweifel Möbel, die häufig vom Stil Louis XVI inspiriert sind, und Dekorationselemente wie majestätische Kronleuchter, Kerzenständer, Spiegel mit Reliefen und Kristallobjekte. Glänzende Flächen und Farben wie Gold, Silber, Bordeaux und Schwarz vermitteln die Essenz des Barock in dieser neuen Interpretation seines verfeinerten und luxuriösen Charakters. Auch die Entwicklung der Herstellungsmethoden und die Perfektionierung von Materialien wie Kunststoffen oder Harzen sind dieser Entwicklung förderlich. Da sie die problemlose Schaffung gebogener Formen ermöglichen, sind sie zu Schlüsselelementen des zeitgenössischen Barockstils und seiner typischsten Charakteristika geworden.

Los movimientos artísticos han ido oscilando como un péndulo entre tendencias opuestas a través de los siglos. En unas épocas se han decantado por la pureza y la simplicidad de las formas, mientras que en otras han elegido la complejidad y la voluptuosidad, como fue el caso del estilo Barroco, imperante en Europa durante el siglo XVII y la primera mitad del XVIII. La necesidad por parte de la iglesia católica, amenazada por el protestantismo, de emocionar y enardecer al pueblo, y la voluntad de las monarquías absolutas de dar muestra de su poder fueron los factores, junto con otros, que provocaron el nacimiento de este estilo caracterizado por sus formas recargadas y ostentosas.

En los últimos años, el mundo de la decoración ha recreado espléndidamente este movimiento en el estilo nuevo barroco, basado en una revisión de sus características, iniciada ya por la moda sobre las pasarelas. La profusión de formas curvas, los excesos en el uso tanto de materiales como de colores y el misterioso juego de claroscuros se han reinterpretado en todo tipo de interiores. También, en ocasiones, es protagonista la misma estructura arquitectónica, como en los palacetes o los edificios de la época que se han rehabilitado con sumo cuidado de rescatar su embriagadora esencia. No obstante, en otros edificios triunfa precisamente el contraste entre la simplicidad y el minimalismo de su estructura con esta decoración neobarroca resplandeciente. Las realizaciones más notables son, sin duda, el mobiliario —inspirado en muchas ocasiones en el estilo Luis XV— y los objetos decorativos, como los majestuosos *chandeliers*, portavelas, espejos con relieves y cristalería. Los brillos y los colores como el dorado, el plateado, el burdeos o el negro consiguen transmitir la esencia del Barroco en esta nueva exhalación de su carácter sofisticado y lujoso. Pero no hay que olvidar que la evolución de los métodos de producción, así como el uso cada vez más frecuente y perfeccionado de materiales como el plástico o las resinas, han favorecido el retorno de la curva, de manera que se ha recuperado este elemento clave del estilo Barroco y su símbolo más representativo.

Au fil des siècles et à l'instar d'un pendule, les mouvements artistiques ont toujours oscillé entre des tendances opposées. A certaines époques, ils ont penchés pour la pureté et la simplicité des formes, choisissant à d'autres moments, la complexité et la volupté, à l'image du style baroque, dominant en Europe au cours du XVIIe siècle et de la première moitié du XVIIIe. La nécessité pour l'Eglise catholique, menacée par le protestantisme, d'émouvoir et d'enflammer le peuple et la volonté des monarques absolus de montrer leur pouvoir, sont certains des facteurs déclencheurs de ce style, caractérisé par ses formes chargées et ostentatoires.

Au cours de ces dernières années, le monde de la décoration a largement recréé ce mouvement avec le style Nouveau Baroque, basé sur une récupération de ses caractéristiques, et, déjà lancé par la mode sur les podiums. L'abondance de formes courbes, l'emploi excessif de matériaux et de couleurs et le mystérieux jeu de clairs-obscurs ont été réinterprétés dans tous les types d'intérieurs. Dans certains cas, c'est la structure architecturale même qui est protagoniste, comme dans les palais et édifices de l'époque, restaurés avec le plus grand soin pour sauvegarder leur essence grisante. Néanmoins, ce qui triomphe dans d'autres édifices, c'est précisément le contraste entre la simplicité et le minimalisme de leur structure et cette décoration néobaroque resplendissante. Les réalisations les plus remarquables sont, sans doute, le mobilier —souvent inspiré du style Louis XV— et les objets décoratifs comme les majestueux lustres, bougeoirs, miroirs sculptés et la verrerie. L'éclat de l'or et l'argent ou les couleurs comme le bordeaux ou le noir permettent de transmettre l'essence même du Baroque dans cette nouvelle exaltation de son caractère sophistiqué et luxueux. Mais rappelons que l'évolution des méthodes de production, alliée à l'emploi toujours plus fréquent et perfectionné de matières comme le plastique ou les résines, ont favorisé le retour de la courbe, récupérant ainsi cet élément clé du style Baroque et son symbole le plus représentatif.

Nel corso dei secoli si è assistito a un continuo e cadenzato altalenare di movimenti artistici che al pari di un pendolo oscillavano tra tendenze opposte. In alcuni periodi hanno optato per la purezza e la semplicità delle forme, mentre in altri hanno scelto la complessità e la voluttuosità, come è stato il caso dello stile Barocco, imperante in Europa durante il XVII secolo e la prima metà del XVIII. La necessità da parte della chiesa cattolica, minacciata dal protestantesimo, di emozionare e di entusiasmare il popolo, e la volontà delle monarchie assolute di fare sfoggio del loro potere furono i fattori che, assieme ad altri, determinarono la nascita di questo stile caratterizzato da forme sovraccariche e ostentatamente vistose. Negli ultimi anni, il mondo dell'arredamento ha ricreato splendidamente questo movimento dando vita allo stile neobarocco, basato su una rivisitazione delle sue caratteristiche, già avviata sulle passerelle nel campo della moda.

La profusione di forme curve, gli eccessi nell'uso sia dei materiali che dei colori e il misterioso gioco dei chiaroscuri sono stati reinterpretati in ogni tipo di interni. In alcune occasioni a farla da protagonista è anche la stessa struttura architettonica, come nei palazzi o edifici dell'epoca che sono stati accuratamente ristrutturati con la voluta intenzione di recuperare la loro inebriante essenza. Ciò nonostante, in altri edifici trionfa precisamente il contrasto tra la semplicità e il minimalismo della loro struttura e un raggiante arredamento neobarocco. Le realizzazioni più riuscite sono senza dubbio la mobilia —ispirata molte volte allo stile Luigi XV— e gli oggetti di arredo come i maestosi *chandelier*, portacandele, specchi con rilievi e cristalleria. Le lucentezze e i colori come l'oro, l'argento, il bordeaux o il nero riescono a trasmettere l'essenza del Barocco in questa nuova emanazione del suo carattere sofisticato e lussuoso. Ma non va dimenticato che l'evoluzione dei metodi di produzione, così come l'uso sempre più frequente e perfezionato dei materiali quali la plastica o le resine, hanno favorito il ritorno della curva, permettendo così il recupero di uno degli elementi chiave, nonché simbolo più rappresentativo del Barocco.

+ ARCH, GIANMARIA TORNO, FERRUCCIO LAVIANI | MILAN, ITALY

Website	www.piuarch.it
Project	Dolce & Gabbana Paris Boutique
Location	Paris, France
Year of completion	2007
Photo credits	Alexis Narodetzky & Gregoire Sevaz

The ladies shop Dolce & Gabbana in Paris has changed address and moved to number 54 of the prestigious Avenue Montaigne. The distinctive elements of the firm, which impregnate their shop interiors throughout the world, have been reproduced once again at this new location. The floors are entirely paved with gray lava rock, the walls clad in black glass and the furniture has a black lacquered finish. This allows the details to be integrated into steel achieving a combination of sophisticated glosses. The lower floor is characterized by the majestic presence of the black glass Venetian chandelier that crowns the center of the space. On the top floor are the VIP rooms where the most exclusive items of clothing and accessories can be found.

Die Damenboutique von Dolce & Gabbana in Paris ist in die Nummer 54 der edlen Avenue Montaigne umgezogen. In diesem neuen Standort wurden alle typischen Elemente der Marke integriert, die die Raumgestaltung der Boutiquen auf der ganzen Welt prägen. Die Böden sind völlig mit grauem Lavagestein bedeckt, die Wände mit schwarzem Glas verkleidet und die Möbel haben schwarz lackierte Oberflächen. Durch die Integration von Stahlelementen wurde eine glanzvolle Kreation geschaffen. Im Erdgeschoss hängt ein majestätischer venezianischer, schwarzer Kronleuchter mitten im Raum. Im Obergeschoss liegen die VIP-Säle mit den exklusivsten Kleidungsstücken und Accessoires.

La tienda de mujer de Dolce & Gabbana en París ha cambiado de dirección y se ha mudado al número 54 de la prestigiosa Avenue Montaigne. En esta nueva ubicación se han reproducido una vez más los elementos distintivos de la firma, que impregnan los interiores de sus tiendas en todo el mundo. Los suelos están completamente pavimentados con piedra de lava gris, las paredes se hallan recubiertas de cristal negro y los muebles tienen un acabado en negro lacado. Se logra así integrar los detalles en acero y se consigue una combinación de sofisticados brillos. La planta inferior se caracteriza por la majestuosidad del *chandelier* veneciano en cristal negro, que corona el centro del espacio. En la planta superior se encuentran las salas VIP, donde se hallan las prendas y complementos más exclusivos.

La boutique de femme de Dolce & Gabbana à Paris a changé d'adresse : elle a déménagé au numéro 54 de la prestigieuse Avenue Montaigne. Dans ce nouvel emplacement, on retrouve, une fois de plus, les caractéristiques de l'enseigne qui imprègnent les intérieurs de ses boutiques du monde entier. Les sols sont entièrement carrelés avec une pierre de lave grise, les murs habillés de verre noir et les meubles dotés d'une finition noire laquée. Cela permet d'intégrer les détails en acier et d'obtenir une combinaison de brillants élégants. L'étage inférieur se caractérise par la majesté du lustre vénitien en cristal noir qui couronne le cœur de l'espace. Le niveau supérieur accueille les salles VIP où l'on découvre les habits et accessoires les plus exclusifs.

La boutique per donna di Dolce & Gabbana a Parigi ha cambiato indirizzo e si è trasferita al numero 54 della prestigiosa Avenue Montaigne. In questa nuova ubicazione sono stati riprodotti ancora una volta gli elementi distintivi della griffe, che caratterizzano gli interni dei suoi negozi in tutto il mondo. A terra la pavimentazione è interamente di pietra lavica grigia, le pareti sono ricoperte di cristallo nero e i mobili presentano una finitura in nero laccato. I dettagli in acciaio, perfettamente integrati, creano una combinazione raffinata di attraenti lucentezze. Al piano inferiore si fa notare un maestoso *chandelier* veneziano in cristallo nero, che corona il centro dello spazio. In quello superiore trovano posto le sale VIP, che accolgono gli abiti e gli accessori più esclusivi.

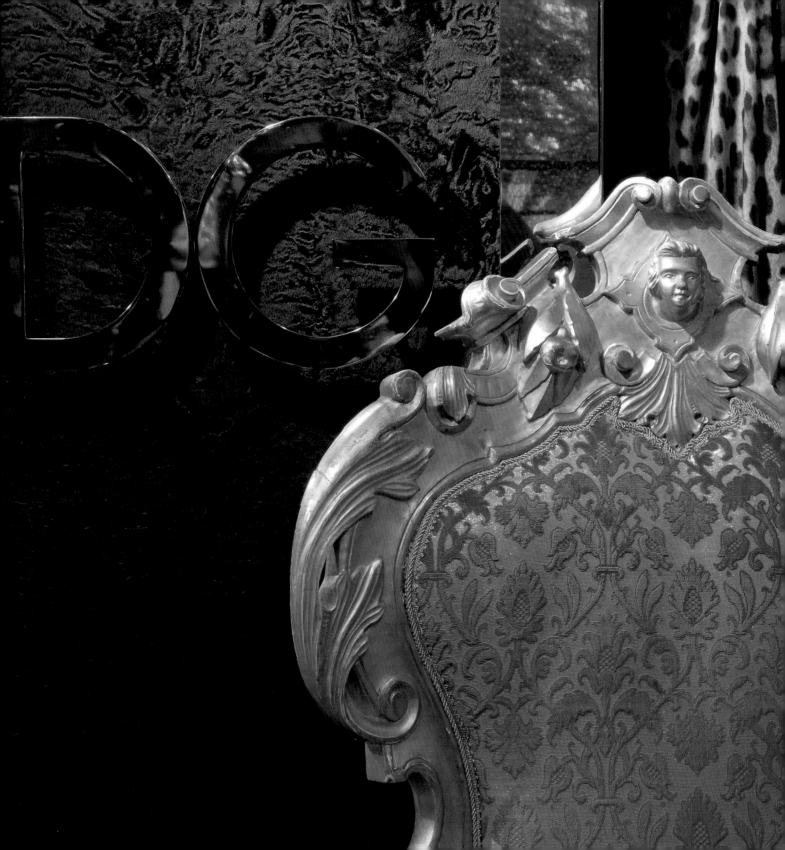

+ ARCH, GIANMARIA TORNO, FERRUCCIO LAVIANI | MILAN, ITALY

Website	www.piuarch.it
Project	Gold by Dolce & Gabbana
Location	Milan, Italy
Year of completion	2006
Photo credits	Ruy Teixeira

The color gold has always been synonymous with luxury and sophistication and this is precisely why Domenico Dolce and Stefano Gabbana, Dolce & Gabbana, christened their first restaurant in Italy "Gold". Studio+Arch, run by Ferruccio Laviani and Gianmaria Torno, took on the project; however, the couturiers were also involved in the interior design of this restaurant which reflects the essence of the fashion house. Its 16,000 ft^2 is divided into two levels: a café, bistro and bar are located on the first floor and an exclusive night time restaurant is housed on the second floor. The marble work and oak floors share the spotlight with metallic and reflective materials such as brass and glass — the luminosity of which enhances the gold colorings of the space. Gold's menu boasts high class Italian cuisine with a mediterranean flavour.

Gold stand schon immer für Luxus. Deshalb tauften Domenico Dolce und Stefano Gabbana ihr erstes Restaurant in Italien, gestaltet von dem Architekturstudio Studio+Arch (Ferruccio Laviani und Gianmaria Torno), Gold. Die Modemacher selbst nahmen aktiv auf die Gestaltung Einfluss, so dass diese die Essenz der Marke widerspiegelt. Die 1500 m^2 große Fläche liegt auf zwei Ebenen; auf der ersten Etage befinden sich das Café, das Bistro und die Bar, auf der zweiten Etage ein exklusives, nur abends geöffnetes Restaurant. Überwiegend wurden die Materialien Marmor und Gold in Kombination mit metallischen, reflektierenden Elementen aus Messing und Glas verwendet, deren Leuchtkraft die goldenen Töne des Lokals unterstreicht. Im Restaurant Gold wird italienische Küche mit den hochwertigen Zutaten des Mittelmeers angeboten.

El color dorado ha sido siempre sinónimo de lujo y sofisticación, y por este motivo Domenico Dolce y Stefano Gabbana, Dolce & Gabbana, han bautizado así su primer restaurante en Italia: Gold. Ha sido proyectado por Studio+Arch, de Ferruccio Laviani y Gianmaria Torno, aunque los modistos participaron también en el diseño del interiorismo de este local que refleja la esencia de la firma. Sus 1500 m^2 se dividen en dos plantas: en el primer nivel se encuentran un café, un bistró y un bar; en el segundo piso se ha ubicado un exclusivo restaurante que abre sólo por la noche. El mármol y el parqué de roble comparten protagonismo con materiales metálicos y reflectantes, como el latón o el cristal, cuya luminosidad ensalza los tonos dorados del local. El menú de Gold ofrece cocina italiana, con ingredientes de alta calidad propios de la dieta mediterránea.

La couleur or a toujours été synonyme de luxe et sophistication. C'est pourquoi Domenico Dolce et Stefano Gabbana, Dolce & Gabbana, ont baptisé leur premier restaurant en Italie : « Gold ». Il a été conçu par le Studio+Arch, de Ferruccio Laviani et Gianmaria Torno, mais le design intérieur de cet établissement porte également le sceau des couturiers, reflétant ainsi l'esprit de la maison de couture. Ses 1500 m^2 se répartissent sur deux étages : le premier niveau héberge un café, un bistrot et un bar, le deuxième étage accueille un restaurant exclusif qui n'ouvre que la nuit. Marbre et parquet en chêne s'affichent en protagonistes aux côtés de matériaux métalliques et réflecteurs comme le laiton ou le verre dont la luminosité exalte les tons or du local. Au Gold, la carte fait honneur à la cuisine italienne, riche d'ingrédients de grande qualité, typiques de l'art culinaire méditerranéen.

Il colore oro è stato sempre sinonimo di lusso e raffinatezza e per questo motivo Domenico Dolce e Stefano Gabbana, Dolce & Gabbana, hanno battezzato così il loro primo ristorante in Italia: Gold. Sebbene sia stato progettato da Studio+Arch di Francesco Laviani e Gianmaria Torno, anche i due stilisti hanno partecipato al disegno degli interni di questo locale che rispecchia l'essenza del loro marchio. I suoi 1500 m^2 si dividono in due piani: a livello strada si trovano un caffè, un bistrò e un bar; il secondo piano è occupato da un esclusivo ristorante che apre soltanto di sera. Il marmo e il parquet di rovere dividono il protagonismo con materiali metallici riflettenti come l'ottone o il vetro, la cui luminosità risalta i toni dorati del locale. Il menu di Gold offre piatti di cucina italiana, con ingredienti di alta qualità, tipici della dieta mediterranea.

+ ARCH, GIANMARIA TORNO, FERRUCCIO LAVIANI | MILAN, ITALY

Website	www.piuarch.it
Project	Metropol by Dolce & Gabbana
Location	Milan, Italy
Year of completion	2006
Photo credits	Andrea Martiradonna

This historic Milan cinema, built at the end of the 1940's, has been restored to all its former glory with the creation of a multi functional space. The fashion designers Dolce & Gabbana were in charge of the new image and have left their particular hallmark in a sophisticated architectural fusion of elegant lines and shapes, with Mediterranean materials such as basalt stone and exquisite finishes. The eye-catching facade leads into the hall which features an enormous chandelier. Magnificent staircases and labyrinth steps lead inside to a baroque inspired lounge and room reserved for social and cultural events, as well as the catwalks where the designers can show off their collections.

Dieses historische Kino in Mailand, erbaut gegen Ende der Vierzigerjahre, wurde mit großem Respekt für seine Originalstruktur renoviert, um einen vielseitig verwendbaren Raum zu schaffen. Verantwortlich für die neue Gestaltung waren die Designer Dolce & Gabbana, die in einer edlen architektonischen Fusion eleganter Linien und Formen, luxuriöser und erlesener Materialien wie Basaltgestein hier ihren eigenen, typischen Stil entwickelt haben. Zunächst fällt die schöne Fassade auf, dann die Halle, in der ein riesiger Kronleuchter hängt. Große Freitreppen und labyrinthische Treppengehäuse führen ins Innere mit einem barock inspirierten Salon, einem Saal für soziale und kulturelle Veranstaltungen und zwei Laufstegen, auf denen die Modemacher ihre Kollektionen zeigen.

Este histórico cine milanés, construido a finales de los años cuarenta, se ha renovado en todo su esplendor con respeto de su estructura original para crear un espacio multiusos. Los encargados de idear su nueva imagen han sido los diseñadores Dolce & Gabbana, quienes han impreso su sello particular en una sofisticada fusión arquitectónica de líneas y volúmenes elegantes, materiales mediterráneos como la piedra basáltica y acabados exquisitos. La vistosa fachada deja paso al hall, presidido por un chandelier enorme. Escalinatas magníficas y escaleras laberínticas conducen al interior, donde se encuentra un salón de inspiración barroca y una sala que acogerá actos sociales y culturales, así como las pasarelas en las que los diseñadores mostrarán sus colecciones.

Ce cinéma milanais historique, construit à la fin des années quarante, a été restauré dans toute sa splendeur, tout en respectant sa structure originale pour créer un espace polyvalent. Les designers Dolce & Gabbana, chargés de réaliser sa nouvelle image, ont imprimé leur sceau personnel dans une fusion architecturale sophistiquée de lignes et volumes élégants, de matériaux méditerranéens, comme la pierre de basalte et de finitions exquises. La façade tape-à-l'œil cède le pas au hall, dominé par un énorme lustre. Perrons splendides et escaliers labyrinthiques mènent à l'intérieur où se trouvent un salon d'inspiration baroque et une salle qui accueillent des évènements sociaux et culturels, à l'instar des podiums où les designers font défiler leurs collections.

Questa storica sala cinematografica milanese della fine degli anni Quaranta è stata ristrutturata in tutta la sua magnificenza e nel rispetto delle strutture originali per creare uno spazio multiuso. L'idea di questo nuovo e grandioso progetto è stata curata dagli stilisti Dolce & Gabbana che hanno impresso il loro marchio particolare in una raffinata fusione architettonica dalle linee e volumi eleganti, e materiali mediterranei come la pietra basaltica e il vetro opalino nero. La vistosa facciata dà accesso alla hall, presieduta da un enorme chandelier. Rifiniture accuratissime e scalinate magnifiche conducono all'interno, dove si trova un salone di ispirazione barocca e una sala destinata ad accogliere eventi socio-culturali, nonché le sfilate per mostrare le ultime collezioni della maison.

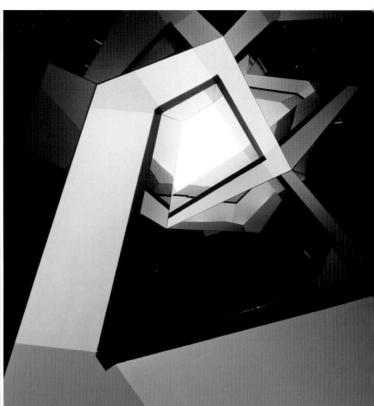

ADD + ARQUITECTURA XAVIER CLARAMUNT | BARCELONA, SPAIN

Website   www.xclaramunt.com
Project   Chic & Basic Born
Location   Barcelona, Spain
Year of completion 2006
Photo credits   Rafael Vargas

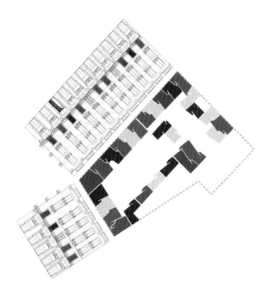

Cherry red? Sea blue? Or emerald green? The Chic & Basic hotel in the fashionable Born neighbourhood of Barcelona leaves the decision up to the guest. At the touch of a button LED lights alter the color of the room and flood it with the optimum ambience for every occasion. This innovative system enhances the magic which this hotel exudes through its high ceilings adorned with mouldings complemented by the Mediterranean and urban influence of the contemporary and baroque furniture. Isabeline sofas, leather and velvet all work in contrast with the white colored round minimalist pieces and technological materials.

Lieber ein leidenschaftliches Rot, das Grün der Hoffnung oder ein gelassenes Gelb? Das Hotel Chic & Basic im Modeviertel von Barcelona El Born lässt den Gast die Farbe seines Zimmers selbst wählen. Durch einen einfachen Knopfdruck verändern Leds den Farbton des Raums und schaffen für jeden Moment die ideale Umgebung. Dieses neuartige System verstärkt noch die Magie dieses Hotels, dessen Architektur durch hohe Stuckdecken geprägt ist und in dessen Räumen mediterran und urban inspirierte, barocke und zeitgenössische Möbel stehen. Elisabethanische Sofas, Leder und Samt bilden einen Kontrast zu minimalistischen und abgerundeten Elementen, zu der Farbe Weiß und technologischen Materialien.

¿Rojo pasión, verde esperanza o, mejor, un azul sereno? El hotel Chic & Basic situado en el Born, barrio de moda de Barcelona, propone que sea el cliente quien escoja y varíe el color de su estancia. Con un simple botón, unos LED cambian el tono de la habitación y la inundan con el ambiente óptimo para cada momento. Este sistema innovador acrecienta la magia que desprende el hotel, cuya arquitectura de techos altos adornados con molduras se complementa con la inspiración mediterránea y urbana del mobiliario barroco y contemporáneo. Sofás isabelinos, piel y terciopelo contrastan con piezas minimalistas y redondeadas, de color blanco y materiales tecnológicos.

Rouge passion, vert espérance ou, mieux encore, un bleu clair? L'hôtel Chic & Basic situé dans le Born, quartier branché de Barcelone, propose au client de choisir et varier la couleur de sa chambre à son gré. D'un simple bouton, des LEDs changent la couleur de la chambre et la plonge dans l'ambiance idéale selon le moment. Ce système innovateur exalte la magie que dégage l'hôtel dont l'architecture des hauts plafonds, décorés de moulures, s'agrémente de l'inspiration méditerranéenne et urbaine du mobilier baroque et contemporain. Divans élisabéthains, cuir et velours contrastent avec les éléments blancs, minimalistes et arrondis et le matériel technologique.

Rosso passione, verde speranza o ancora meglio, un blu sereno? L'hotel Chic & Basic situato nel Born, quartiere alla moda di Barcellona, è in grado di far scegliere e variare ai loro clienti l'abbinamento cromatico della camera dove soggiorneranno. Basta solo premere un pulsante, ed alcuni LED cambiano la tonalità della stanza creandovi un'atmosfera che si adatta ad ogni momento. Un sistema davvero innovativo che incrementa l'alone di magia di questo singolare hotel. Dal punto di vista architettonico, ai soffitti alti e decorati con modanature si abbinano dei mobili barocchi e contemporanei di ispirazione mediterranea ed urbana. Divani dal colore isabellino, pelle e velluto abbinati ad elementi minimalisti e dalle forme arrotondate, di colore bianco e materiali tecnologici.

Chic&basic is different. It's new. It's a concept. It's simple, it's smart, it's surprising. It's open-minded, it's cool. It's fresh ideas. It's naughty. Is it possible? Yes, it is. It's contemporary. It's comfortable. It's a nightlife guide. It's easy to check in, it's easy to check out. It's just easy. It's fusion. It's cross-culture. It's Spanish, it's English, it's French, it's bla, bla, bla. It's like... It's Chic, it's Basic, that's what it is.

chic&basic®

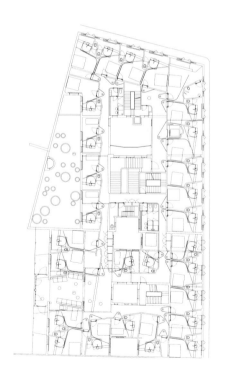

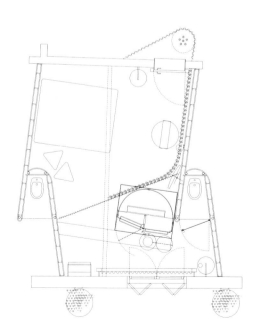

ANA ROS DESIGN | BARCELONA, SPAIN

Website	www.anarosbcn.com
Project	Ana Ros Exhibition/Casa Decor 2004
Location	Barcelona, Spain
Year of completion	2004
Photo credits	Ana Ros

This reproduction of a house was designed by the interior designer Ana Ros for the 2004 Casa Decor exhibition. Each of the pieces and accessories have been carefully selected in order to create a harmonius space in which the author's hallmark is evident: a marked neoclassic chic style with romantic touches. The color white blends with mauve and varying shades of lilac in the common zones as well as in the bedroom. A magnificent chaise longue proudly stands in the lounge in front of the embossed fireplace. The color gold, a central theme in rest of the rooms, is also used in the bathroom where it is combined with black and together with the mirrors creates a sophisticated atmosphere.

Diese Nachbildung einer Wohnung wurde von der Raumgestalterin Ana Ros für die Ausstellung Casa Decor 2004 entworfen. Jedes Element und Accessoire wurde sorgfältig ausgewählt, um einen harmonischen Raum im Stil der Schöpferin zu schaffen: ein betont neoklassischer, schicker Stil mit romantischen Elementen. Die Farbe Weiß wird mit Mauve kombiniert und mit verschiedenen Lilatönen in den Gemeinschaftsbereichen und im Schlafzimmer. Eine wundervolle Chaiselongue beherrscht das Wohnzimmer vor einem mit vergoldeten Reliefs dekorierten Kamin. Die Farbe Gold ist auch in den übrigen Räumen und im Bad in Kombination mit Schwarz zu finden. Im Bad sorgen Spiegel für eine elegante Atmosphäre.

Esta reproducción de una vivienda fue diseñada por la interiorista Ana Ros para la exposición Casa Decor 2004. Cada pieza y cada complemento se han escogido cuidadosamente para lograr un espacio armónico en el que domina el sello de su autora: un marcado estilo neoclásico chic con pinceladas románticas. El color blanco se mezcla con el malva y distintas tonalidades lilas tanto en las zonas comunes como en el dormitorio. Una magnífica *chaise longue* preside el salón, frente a la chimenea adornada con relieves. El color dorado, presente también en el resto de las salas, se utiliza también en el baño combinado con el negro y junto con los espejos da lugar a una atmósfera sofisticada.

Cette reproduction d'une demeure a été conçue par l'architecte d'intérieur Ana Ros pour l'exposition Casa Decor 2004. Objets et accessoires ont été soigneusement choisis pour obtenir un espace harmonieux marqué du sceau de sa créatrice : un cadre de style néoclassique chic ponctué de touches romantiques. Le blanc se mêle au mauve et à un camaïeu de violet dans les zones communes comme dans la chambre à coucher. Une superbe chaise longue trône dans le salon, face à la cheminée décorée de reliefs. Le doré, également présent dans le reste des salles, s'utilise aussi dans la salle de bains où, combiné au noir et aux miroirs, il engendre une atmosphère sophistiquée.

Questa riproduzione di un'abitazione è stata allestita dalla *interior designer* Ana Ros per la mostra Casa Decor 2004. Ogni pezzo e accessorio è stato accuratamente selezionato per ottenere uno spazio armonico in cui si nota il marchio della sua autrice: un marcato stile neoclassico chic con pennellate romantiche. Il colore bianco si mescola con il malva e diverse tonalità di lilla sia nelle zone comuni che nella camera da letto. Una magnifica *chaise-longue* presiede il salotto, di fronte al camino ornato di rilievi. Il colore oro, presente anche nel resto delle sale, si abbina al nero nella sala da bagno dove assieme agli specchi crea una raffinata atmosfera.

ATELIER MENDINI, IGLIS ZORZI | MILAN, ITALY

Website	www.ateliermendini.it
Project	Byblos Art Hotel Villa Amistà
Location	Verona, Italy
Year of completion	2005
Photo credits	Henri del Olmo

Art, design and fashion merge in this picturesque hotel located in a 15th century Italian villa near Verona. The Byblos Art Hotel Villa Amista was conceived as a permanent art exhibition and all its rooms and lounges contain works of art by contemporary designers. This has led to a curious combination within the original structure which has been restored and given a peculiar aesthetic through an explosion of color. Most of the furniture and decorative objects involve shapes and styles from the 17th century albeit customized with materials and colors in harmony with the global aesthetic of the hotel. Each room however has its own color scheme and personality.

Kunst, Design und Mode treffen in diesem malerischen Hotel in einer italienischen Villa aus dem 15. Jh. in der Nähe von Verona aufeinander. Das Byblos Art Hotel Villa Amistà wurde wie eine permanente Kunstausstellung angelegt, so dass man in allen Räumen und Salons Werke zeitgenössischer Künstler bewundern kann. Für diese Initiative war das Gebäude prädestiniert: Der restaurierten Originalstruktur gab man durch die vielfarbige Gestaltung eine ganz besondere Ästhetik. Ein großer Teil der Möbel und Dekorationselemente greifen typische Formen und Stilelemente des 17. Jh. auf, obwohl sie in ihren Stoffen und Farben auch an die globale Ästhetik des Hotels angepasst wurden. Jeder Raum hat seine eigenen Farbtöne und Charakteristika.

Arte, diseño y moda confluyen en este pintoresco hotel ubicado en una villa italiana del siglo XV, cerca de Verona. El Byblos Art Hotel Villa Amistà se ha concebido como una exposición de arte permanente, por lo que en todas sus estancias y salones se han dispuesto obras de arte de diseñadores contemporáneos. Esta iniciativa ha supuesto una curiosa combinación con la estructura original de la construcción, que se ha restaurado y a la que se ha dotado de una estética peculiar mediante una explosión de color. Gran parte del mobiliario y de los objetos decorativos rescatan las formas y el estilo del siglo XVII, aunque customizados con telas y colores acordes con la estética global del hotel. Cada estancia, además, tiene su propia personalidad y colorido.

Art, design et mode se rejoignent dans cet hôtel pittoresque situé dans une ville italienne du XVe siècle, près de Vérone. Le Byblos Art Hotel Villa Amistà est conçu comme une exposition d'art permanente, chaque pièce accueillant des œuvres d'art de designers contemporains. Cette initiative engendre une curieuse alliance avec la structure originale de la construction, qui depuis sa restauration, revêt une esthétique particulière par le biais d'une explosion de couleurs. Une grande partie du mobilier et des objets de décoration exalte les formes du style XVIIe siècle, tout en étant customisés avec des tissus et des couleurs en harmonie avec l'esthétique générale de l'hôtel. En outre, chaque pièce possède une personnalité unique et ses propres coloris.

Arte, design e moda confluiscono in questo pittoresco hotel ubicato in una villa italiana del XV sec., nei pressi di Verona. Il Byblos Art Hotel Villa Amistà è stato concepito come una mostra d'arte permanente per cui in tutte le sue stanze sono state collocate diverse opere d'arte di artisti contemporanei. Questa iniziativa ha significato una curiosa combinazione con la struttura originale dell'edificio, ristrutturata e a cui è stata data un'estetica particolare mediante un'esplosione di colori. Gran parte della mobilia e degli oggetti decorativi riprendono le forme e lo stile del XVII sec., sebbene personalizzati con tele e colori consoni all'estetica globale dell'hotel. Ogni camera, inoltre, è dotata di colori e personalità propri.

BARBOSA SPACE PROJECTS/RICARDO & TINO BARBOSA | OVIEDO, SPAIN

Website	www.barbosasp.com
Project	Casa en Oviedo
Location	Oviedo, Spain
Year of completion	2006
Photo credits	Grapheim

Following the peak of minimalism, the mix of styles and trends with decorative elements such as painted wallpaper and gold leaf details are back in fashion. The Barbosa brothers have restored this house accordingly and have converted it into a unique place. A spiral staircase dominates the house and connects the three floors. In the dining room the color silver is prevalent; grey mosaics reign in the kitchen and service areas, whilst in the bedroom, bright colors are the main theme, such as pink and gold. The chaise longue at the entrance and the bedhead have been upholstered in capitone to evoke the ostentation of the most overelaborate of styles.

Nach dem Triumph des Minimalismus erlebt die Mischung von Stilen und Trends ein Revival, und Dekorationselemente wie Goldplättchen und Tapeten sind erneut gefragt. Die Firma Hermanos Barbosa hat dieses Einfamilienhaus renoviert und es einzigartig gemacht. Jeder Raum hat seine eigene Persönlichkeit. Eine spindelförmige Treppe beherrscht das Bild und verbindet die drei Stockwerke miteinander. Das Speisezimmer ist in der Farbe Silber gestaltet. In der Küche gibt es graues Mosaik, und im Schlafzimmer herrschen kräftige Farben wie Rosa und Gold vor. Sowohl die Chaiselongue am Eingang als auch das Kopfteil des Betts sind mit gestepptem Polster bezogen, um an die Pracht prunkvoller Stile zu erinnern.

Tras el auge del minimalismo, vuelve la mezcla de estilos y tendencias con elementos decorativos tal como el pan de oro o los papeles pintados. Los hermanos Barbosa han rehabilitado esta vivienda unifamiliar siguiendo esta línea y convirtiendo el espacio en el verdadero protagonista, dotando a cada estancia de una personalidad única. Una escalera helicoidal preside la casa y comunica sus tres pisos. En el comedor se ha usado el color plata; en la cocina y las zonas de servicio, el mosaico gris, y en el dormitorio imperan los colores vivos como el rosa y el dorado. Tanto la *chaise longue* de la entrada como el cabezal de la cama han sido tapizados en capitoné, para evocar la ostentación de los estilos más recargados.

Après l'apogée du minimalisme, c'est le retour du mélange des styles et des tendances fortes d'éléments décoratifs tels que la feuille d'or ou les papiers peints. Les frères Barbosa ont restauré cette demeure individuelle en suivant cette ligne et en convertissant l'espace en véritable protagoniste, dotant chaque pièce d'une personnalité unique. Un escalier hélicoïdal, point de mire de la maison, relie ses trois étages. Dans la salle à manger, on a choisi la couleur argent et dans la cuisine et les zones de service, la mosaïque grise. Dans la chambre à coucher, les couleurs vives prédominent, à l'instar du rose ou doré. Que ce soit la chaise longue de l'entrée ou la tête de lit, toutes deux sont capitonnées, évoquant ainsi le côté ostentatoire des styles plus chargés.

Dopo l'auge del minimalismo, ritorna la mescolanza di stili e tendenze con elementi decorativi quali la doratura a foglia d'oro e la carta da parati. I fratelli Barbosa hanno ristrutturato questa abitazione unifamiliare seguendo questa linea, convertendo lo spazio nel vero protagonista e dotando ogni stanza di una personalità unica. Una scala elicoidale presiede la casa e comunica i suoi tre piani. Nella sala da pranzo si è usato il colore argento; nella cucina e nelle zone di servizio il mosaico grigio mentre nella camera da letto predominano i colori vivi come il rosa e il dorato. Sia la *chaise-longue* dell'ingresso che la testata del letto sono stati tappezzati in capitonnè, per evocare l'ostentazione e il lusso degli stili più carichi.

BEHF ARCHITEKTEN | VIENNA, AUSTRIA

Website   www.behf.at
Project   2006Feb01
Location   Vienna, Austria
Year of completion 2006
Photo credits   Bruno Klomfar

Exclusivity and singularity are the parameters for the design of this shop, situated in the heart of Vienna, with views over the Saint Stephen cathedral and the baroque Donner fountain. In the arches which comprise the entrance – part of the historic stone façade of the building – glass and black panels, which can be opened, have been positioned. This play on transparency and illumination is repeated throughout the interior. Despite the simplicity of the principal structure, which creates spacious areas with few features, the decoration achieves a pleasant cosy ambience thanks to the large lamps, translucent curtains and the use of harmonious colour schemes. The dressing rooms have been lined with unusual, wild floral patterns.

Exklusivität und Einzigartigkeit waren die Gestaltungsparameter für dieses Geschäft im Herzen Wiens mit Blick auf den Stefansdom und den barocken Donnerbrunnen. Zwischen den Bögen am Eingang in der historischen Steinfassade des Gebäudes hat man schwarze und gläserne Platten angebracht, die offen bleiben können. So spielte man mit der Idee der Transparenz und Beleuchtung, die sich im Inneren wiederholt. Trotz der einfachen Hauptstruktur, die weite Räume mit wenigen Elementen entstehen lässt, wurde durch die Dekoration eine angenehme und freundliche Atmosphäre geschaffen. Dazu tragen die großen Lampen, die lichtdurchlässigen Gardinen und die harmonische Farbenkombination bei. Die mit Blumen- und Dschungelmustern verkleideten Umkleidekabinen stellen einen interessanten Kontrast dar.

Exclusividad y singularidad son los parámetros de los que parte el diseño de esta tienda, situada en el corazón de Viena, con vistas a la catedral de San Esteban y a la fuente barroca Donner. En los arcos que forman la entrada, insertada en la histórica fachada de piedra del edificio, se han dispuesto paneles negros y de cristal, que pueden quedar abiertos. Se ha jugado así con la idea de transparencia e iluminación que se repite en el interior. A pesar de la simplicidad de la estructura principal, que crea amplios espacios sin apenas elementos, la decoración logra un ambiente agradable y acogedor, gracias a las grandes lámparas, las cortinas translúcidas y el uso de tonos armónicos. En un curioso contraste, los probadores han sido forrados con estampados florales y selváticos.

Exclusivité et singularité sont les paramètres initiaux du design de cette boutique située au cœur de Vienne, avec vues sur la cathédrale de Saint Stephen et la fontaine baroque Donner. Les arcs qui forment l'entrée, insérée dans la façade historique en pierre de l'édifice, accueillent des panneaux noirs et de verre qui peuvent rester ouverts. On a joué avec le concept de transparence et d'éclairage qui se répète à l'intérieur. En dépit de la simplicité de la structure principale qui crée d'amples espaces avec peu d'éléments, la décoration forge une atmosphère agréable et accueillante, grâce aux grandes lampes, aux rideaux translucides et à l'emploi de tons harmonieux. Créant un curieux contraste, les cabines d'essayage ont été doublées d'imprimés floraux et sylvestres.

Esclusività e singolarità sono i parametri da cui parte il design di questo negozio, situato nel cuore di Vienna, con vedute della cattedrale di Santo Stefano e la fontana barocca dello scultore Donner. Negli archi che formano l'ingresso, inserito nella storica facciata di pietra dell'edificio, sono stati disposti dei pannelli neri e di cristallo che possono rimanere aperti. Si è giocato così con l'idea di trasparenza e illuminazione che si ripete anche all'interno. Nonostante la semplicità della struttura principale, l'arredamento dà vita a un ambiente accogliente e piacevole mediante grandi lampade, tende trasparenti e l'uso di toni armonici. In un curioso contrasto, i camerini sono stati rivestiti con stampati floreali e selvatici.

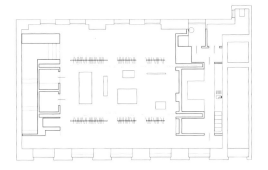

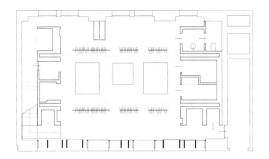

CARLO DAL BIANCO | VICENZA, ITALY

Website   www.carlodalbianco.it
Project   Bisazza Showroom Berlin
Location   Berlin, Germany
Year of completion 2005
Photo credits   Eric Laignel

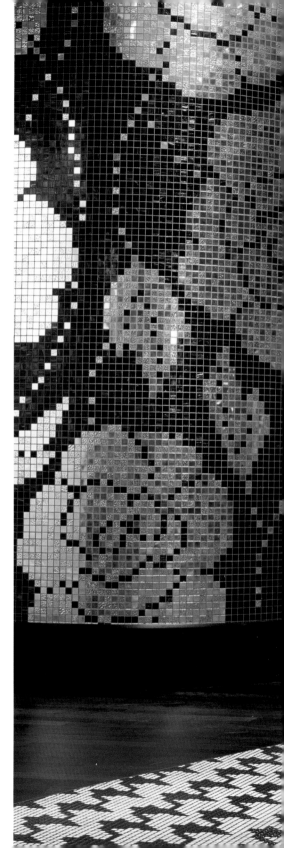

The architect Carlo dal Bianco, head of the Bisazza Design Studio team, has led the creation of the firm's different showrooms which have been launched in the main design capitals, all of which, including this one located in Berlin, are inspired by a luxurious and classic aesthetic. Every surface is decorated with a diffent mosaic design including the walls which separate the rooms. This showroom boasts modern, classic baroque inspired pieces and designs, resulting in a contemporary version of this style.

L'architecte Carlo dal Bianco, à la tête de l'équipe du Bisazza Design Studio, est le créateur des différents showrooms ouverts par la maison de mosaïques dans les principales capitales du design. Tous, comme celui de Berlin, ont été conçus selon une esthétique classique et luxueuse. Chaque surface est revêtue d'un design de mosaïques distinct : un nouveau décor est proposé en fonction des murs qui délimitent chaque pièce. Pour ce showroom, on a choisi des pièces et designs de la collection d'influence Baroque Modern Classic qui propose une récupération contemporaine de ce style.

Der Architekt Carlo dal Bianco, der das Bisazza Design-Studio leitet, war auch der Schöpfer verschiedener Bisazza Showrooms, die in den Hauptstädten des Designs eröffnet worden sind. Diese sind alle – wie auch der Showroom in Berlin – in einem klassisch und luxuriös inspirierten Stil dekoriert. Die Oberflächen sind mit verschiedenen Mosaikmotiven verkleidet und an den Wänden der verschiedenen Räume werden Vorschläge für neue Dekorationsstile gezeigt. Für diesen Showroom wählte man Teile und Muster der barock inspirierten Kollektion ModernClassic, die eine Art zeitgemäße Neuauflage des Barockstils darstellt.

Carlo dal Bianco, alla guida degli architetti del Bisazza Design Studio, ha curato l'allestimento dei vari showroom che la nota azienda veneta di mosaici ha inaugurato nelle principali capitali del design. Tutti gli showroom, come questo situato a Berlino, sono stati concepiti secondo uno stile lussuoso di impronta classica. Ogni superficie è rivestita con un disegno di mosaici diverso e le stesse pareti che delimitano ogni ambiente propongono nuovi modi di decorare. Per questo showroom sono stati scelti pezzi e disegni della collezione di influenza barocca ModernClassic, che propone una rivisitazione di questo stile in chiave contemporanea.

El arquitecto Carlo dal Bianco, que encabeza el equipo de Bisazza Design Studio, ha sido el artífice de los distintos *showrooms* que la casa de mosaicos ha abierto en las principales capitales del diseño. Todos ellos, como éste ubicado en Berlín, se han proyectado bajo la inspiración de una estética clásica y lujosa. Cada superficie está revestida con un diseño de mosaicos distinto y, ya desde las mismas paredes que delimitan cada estancia, se propone una nueva manera de decorar. Para este *showroom* se han escogido piezas y diseños de la colección de influencia barroca ModernClassic, que propone una contemporánea revisión de este estilo.

CHRISTIAN GHION | PARIS, FRANCE

Website   www.christianghion.com
Project   Chantal Thomas Boutique
Location   Paris, France
Year of completion 2004
Photo credits   Roger Casas

The fundamental intention of the project was to translate the spirit of the lingerie designer Chantal Thomas into the design of this space and thus transmit the values of the brand: luxury, femininity, seduction and the desire to be modern. The boutique, situated in the exclusive rue de Saint Honoré in Paris, plays on infinite shades of pink and black with touches of silver. The furniture is inspired by the baroque style in a reinterpretation of sinuous shapes and pretty colors. A large round shaped rug shines on the floor of the shop under the light from the chandelier and the Murano glass wall lamps.

L'idée première du projet est de traduire l'esprit de Chantal Thomas, créatrice de lingerie, dans le design et l'architecture intérieure de cet espace, tout en transmettant les valeurs de l'enseigne : le luxe, la féminité, la séduction et la volonté d'être moderne. La boutique, située à Paris, dans l'exclusive rue de Saint Honoré, joue avec une infinité de nuances roses, le noir et des touches de couleur argent. Le mobilier s'inspire du style baroque, dans une réinterprétation de formes sinueuses et de couleurs affriolantes. Un grand tapis rond brille sur le sol de la boutique, sous la lumière du lustre et des lampes murales en cristal de Murano.

Die bestimmende Idee bei dieser Raumgestaltung war es, die Linie der Lingerie Designerin Chantal Thomas auf die Dekoration zu übertragen und so die Werte der Marke zu vermitteln, nämlich Luxus, Weiblichkeit, Verführung und das Bekenntnis zur Mode. Die Boutique liegt in der exklusiven Rue Saint-Honoré in Paris. In den Räumen spielte man mit verschiedenen Rosanuancen, mit der Farbe Schwarz und einigen Pinselstrichen Silber. Die Möbel sind vom Barockstil inspiriert, eine Art Neuinterpretation mit kurvigen Formen und koketten Farben. Ein großer, runder Teppich liegt auf dem Boden unter dem Licht eines Kronleuchters und einiger Wandlampen aus Muranoglas.

L'intenzione primordiale del progetto è stata quella di tradurre lo spirito della stilista di lingerie Chantal Thomas nel design interno di questo spazio, trasmettendo così i valori del marchio: lusso, femminilità, seduzione e la volontà di essere moderno. La boutique, situata nell'esclusiva Rue de Saint Honoré di Parigi, gioca con infinite tonalità di rosa, con il nero e con pennellate color argento. L'arredamento, ispirato allo stile barocco, presenta una reinterpretazione moderna fatta di forme sinuose e colori accattivanti. A terra il negozio sfoggia un grande tappeto rotondo sotto la luce di uno chandelier e di varie lampade da parete in cristallo di Murano.

La intención primordial del proyecto fue la de traducir el espíritu de la diseñadora de lencería Chantal Thomas en el diseño e interiorismo de este espacio, y de esta manera transmitir los valores de la marca: el lujo, la feminidad, la seducción y la voluntad de ser moderna. La boutique, situada en la exclusiva rue de Saint Honoré de París, juega con infinitas tonalidades de rosa, con el negro y con pinceladas de color plata. El mobiliario está inspirado en el estilo barroco, en una reinterpretación con formas sinuosas y colores coquetos. Una gran alfombra redonda luce en el suelo de la tienda, bajo la luz del chandelier y las lámparas de pared en cristal de Murano.

CRISTINA GABÁS (INTERIOR DESIGNER) | BARCELONA, SPAIN

Project   Neri Hotel
Location   Barcelona, Spain
Year of completion 2003
Photo credits   Habitat Hotels, Yael Pincus

4 SOLARIUM

3 HAB. I ROOM
301-306

2 HAB. I ROO
201-209

1 HAB. I ROO
101-107

0 LOBBY
BIBLIOTEC
RESTAURAN

The gothic quarter of Barcelona is an historic gem. The hotel Neri is located in the heart of this spectacular setting, housed in an 18th century palace which blends the existing structure and original elements with contemporary interior design. Here time seems to stand still and sophistication and glamour reign. In the interior courtyard the walls and staircase are made of stone, as are the arches which separate the bar from the tables in the restaurant. The velvet and iridescent materials of the furniture recreate the luxury that was doubtless prevalent in the same building centuries ago.

Le quartier gothique de Barcelone regorge d'histoire dans ses moindres recoins. C'est dans ce cadre incomparable de la ville que se situe l'Hôtel Neri, installé dans un petit palais du XVIIIe siècle qui exalte ses signes d'identité originaux en les alliant à des intérieurs au design contemporain. Dans ce lieu, où le temps semble s'être arrêté, la sophistication et le glamour semblent évidents. Dans le patio intérieur, la pierre, matière qui revêt murs et perron, est également utilisée dans le restaurant, sous forme d'arcs qui séparent le bar des tables. Le velours et les autres tissus chatoyant du mobilier parviennent à recréer le luxe, certainement déjà à l'honneur dans cette construction, des siècles auparavant.

Im gotischen Viertel von Barcelona spürt man die Vergangenheit in jedem Winkel. In einem Palast aus dem 18. Jh. befindet sich in dieser wundervollen Umgebung das Hotel Neri, dessen Originalstruktur mit einer zeitgenössischen Innenarchitektur kombiniert wurde. Hier scheint die Zeit stillzustehen, und die Atmosphäre ist von Noblesse und Glamour geprägt. Die Wände und die Freitreppe des Innenhofes bestehen aus Naturstein, der auch im Restaurant zu finden ist, dessen Bögen die Bar von den Tischen trennen. Die mit Samt und changierenden Stoffen verkleideten Möbel lassen den Luxus wieder aufleben, den man sicher Jahrhunderte vorher auch schon in diesem Gebäude vorfand.

Il quartiere gotico di Barcellona trasuda storia da ogni sua pietra ed angolo. In questa raccolta e silenziosa piazzetta sorge l'Hotel Neri, all'interno di un palazzo del XVIII secolo completamente ristrutturato che accoglie interni dal design contemporaneo. Tutte le camere sono in sintonia con la serenità ed eleganza delle aree comuni dell'hotel. Il materiale più adoperato è la pietra, presente nel cortile interno, nella scalinata ed anche nel ristorante, dove forma gli archi che separano il bancone dai tavoli. Il velluto e alcune stoffe cangianti usate per l'arredamento creano un ambiente lussuoso che di certo era presente in questa costruzione alcuni secoli fa.

El barrio gótico de Barcelona rebosa historia en cada uno de sus rincones. En este marco incomparable de la ciudad se encuentra el Hotel Neri, situado en un palacete del siglo XVIII que pone de manifiesto sus señas de identidad originales combinadas con unos interiores de diseño contemporáneo. En este lugar, el tiempo parece detenerse y la sofisticación y el *glamour* se hacen evidentes. En el patio interior, la piedra es el material de las paredes y la escalinata, también utilizada en el restaurante, donde forma los arcos que separan la barra de las mesas. El terciopelo y algunos tejidos tornasolados en el mobiliario logran recrear un lujo que, seguro, también albergaba esta misma construcción siglos atrás.

4 SOLARIUM

3 HAB. ROOMS
   301-306

2 HAB. ROOMS
   201-209

1 HAB. ROOMS
   101-107

0 LOBBY
   BIBLIOTECA LIBRARY
   RESTAURANT

RESTAURANTE

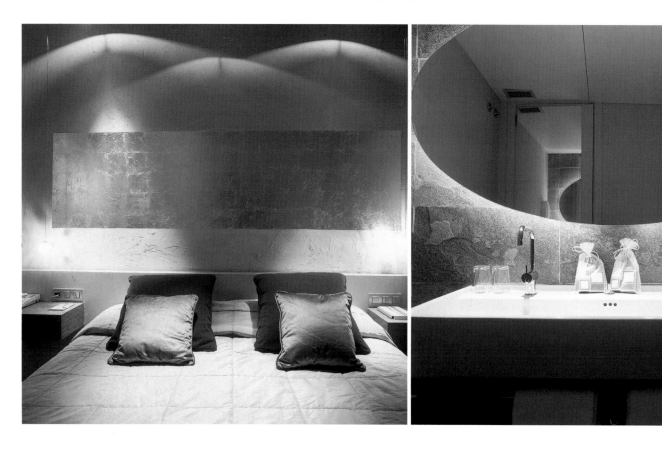

DAVID COLLINS STUDIO | LONDON, UNITED KINGDOM

Website	www.davidcollins.com
Project	Petrus Restaurant
Location	London, United Kingdom
Year of completion	2006
Photo credits	David Collins Studio

Petrus, housed in London's Berkeley Hotel, has become one of the city's most acclaimed restaurants. It is named after the chateau in the Bordeaux wine region of France renowned for producing one of the world's finest wines. The decoration, the work of interior designer David Collins, reproduces the blush of the wine through the use of colors and textures combined with lacquered surfaces and mirrors which reflect the light. The windows are partially covered by French style latticework. Their circular shapes bring a truly personal touch to the place.

Das Petrus im Londoner Hotel Berkeley ist eines der beliebtesten Restaurants der Stadt. Der Name leitet sich von dem berühmten „Château" in der Weinregion Bordeaux ab, wo die besten Weine der Welt gekeltert werden sollen. Für die Dekoration war der Designer David Collins verantwortlich. Er reproduzierte die Töne des Bordeauxweins in den Farben und Texturen, die er mit Spiegeln und lackierten Flächen kombinierte, in denen das Licht reflektiert. Die Fenster sind teilweise mit Strukturen bedeckt, die französische Jalousien nachbilden. Dieses Detail mit seinen runden Formen wiederholt sich im ganzen Restaurant und wird zu einem ganz persönlichen Ausdrucksmittel.

El Petrus, ubicado en el hotel londinense Berkeley, se ha convertido en uno de los restaurantes más aclamados de la ciudad. Su nombre proviene del famoso *château* situado en la región vinícola de Burdeos y conocido por producir uno de los mejores vinos del mundo. La decoración, llevada a cabo por el diseñador David Collins, reproduce claramente en sus colores y texturas los tonos del vino de Burdeos, combinados con espejos y superficies lacadas que reflejan la luz. Las ventanas se han cubierto parcialmente con unas estructuras a modo de celosía de inspiración francesa. Este detalle se repite en todo el restaurante y aporta un sello muy personal gracias a sus formas circulares.

Le Petrus, situé dans l'hôtel londonien de Berkeley, est devenu l'un des restaurants les plus prisés de la cité. Son nom vient du fameux château situé dans la région vinicole de Bordeaux, connue pour produire l'un des meilleurs vins du monde. La décoration, œuvre du designer David Collins, reproduit clairement dans ses couleurs et textures les tons du vin de Bordeaux, en les combinant à des miroirs et surfaces laquées qui réfléchissent la lumière. Les fenêtres ont été partiellement habillées d'une structure ressemblant à des jalousies d'inspiration française. Ce détail se répète dans tout le restaurant et grâce à ses formes circulaires, il y imprime un sceau très personnel.

Il Petrus, aperto all'interno dell'hotel londinese Berkeley, è diventato uno dei ristoranti più famosi della capitale britannica. Il nome proviene dal celeberrimo Chateau Petrus, uno dei più cari vini al mondo, prodotto nella regione vinicola di Bordeaux. L'arredamento, a cura del designer David Collins, riproduce chiaramente nei colori e le texture i toni del vino di Bordeaux, ben abbinati a specchi e superfici laccate che riflettono la luce. Le finestre sono state rivestite parzialmente con dei serramenti a gelosia di ispirazione francese. Questa soluzione si ripropone in tutto il ristorante e grazie alle sue forme circolari dà un tocco molto personale.

DAVID HICKS | SOUTH YARRA, VICTORIA, AUSTRALIA

Website	www.davidhicks.com.au
Project	Evé Night Club
Location	Melbourne, Australia
Year of completion	2005
Photo credits	Trevor Mein / Meinphoto

This Melbourne club is characterized by the aesthetics of the seventies and early eighties combined with the glamour of the baroque style. Housed in the basement, this club transports those who enter towards a new world which unfolds in different ambiences. In the Dragon Bar, a large glass dragon shaped chandelier takes pride of place amongst the glitter and exotic wallpaper. Bar Tiger offers a more sensual and sophistacated atmosphere with its silver mirrors and Roccocco armchairs. The Garden Bar is decorated in gold where even the bars themselves are of golden colorings which separate it from the central area. The dance floor extends outwards infront of the bars and is made of glass panels which change color and reflect the lights onto the ceiling.

Details, die von der Ästhetik der Siebziger- und der beginnenden Achtzigerjahre inspiriert sind, vermischen sich mit dem Glamour barocker Elemente, die diesen Club in Melbourne charakterisieren. Wenn man das Lokal im Untergeschoss betritt, ist es, als ob man eine neue Welt entdeckt, die sich in verschiedenen Räumen öffnet. In der Bar Dragon begrüßen ein großer, drachenförmiger, glitzernder Kronleuchter und exotische Tapeten den Besucher. Edler und sinnlicher wirkt die Bar Tiger mit silbernen Spiegeln und Rokokosesseln. In der Bar Garden spielt die Farbe Gold die Hauptrolle; vom zentralen Bereich ist sie durch goldene Schranken abgetrennt. Davor erstreckt sich die Tanzfläche, deren Boden aus Glasscheiben besteht, die die Farbe wechseln und sich an der Decke widerspiegeln läßt.

Detalles inspirados en la estética de los setenta y principios de los ochenta se mezclan con el *glamour* de notas barrocas que caracteriza a este club de Melbourne. Situado en un sótano, el local transporta a quien entra en él hacia un nuevo mundo que se despliega en diferentes ambientes. En el bar Dragon, un gran *chandelier* de cristal en forma de dragón da la bienvenida entre un juego de destellos y exóticos papeles de pared. Un *look* más sofisticado y sensual es el del bar Tiger, con espejos en plata y butacas rococó, en tanto que el color dorado es el protagonista del bar Garden, franqueado por barras áureas que lo separan del área central. Delante, la pista de baile se extiende en un suelo formado por paneles de cristal que cambian de color y se refleja en el techo.

Détails inspirés de l'esthétique des années soixante-dix et débuts des années quatre-vingt se mêlent au glamour des touches baroques qui définissent ce club de Melbourne. Situé dans un sous-sol, l'établissement entraîne quiconque y entre dans un nouvel univers qui s'ouvre sur diverses ambiances. Dans le bar Dragon, un grand lustre de verre en forme de dragon accueille le client au milieu d'un jeu de scintillements et de papiers muraux exotiques. Le bar Tiger affiche un *look* plus sophistiqué et sensuel, avec ses miroirs d'argent et fauteuils rococo, tandis que la couleur or est la protagoniste du bar Garden, doté de comptoirs en or qui le séparent de l'aire centrale. Devant, la piste de danse s'étend sur des panneaux de verre qui changent de couleur et se reflètent dans le plafond.

Particolari ispirati all'estetica degli anni 70 e agli inizi degli 80 si mescolano al *glamour* di note barocche che caratterizza questo club di Melbourne. Situato al piano interrato, il locale trasporta chi vi entra verso un nuovo mondo che si spiega in ambienti diversi. Nel bar Dragon, un grande *chandelier* di cristallo a forma di drago dà il benvenuto in mezzo a un gioco di luccichii ed esotiche carte da parati. Un *look* più sofisticato e sensuale contraddistingue il bar Tiger, con specchi in argento e poltrone rococò; il colore oro, invece, è il protagonista del bar Garden, formato da banconi aurei che lo separano dall'area centrale. Davanti, la pista da ballo si stende su un pavimento composto da pannelli di cristallo che cambiano colore e che si riflette sul soffitto.

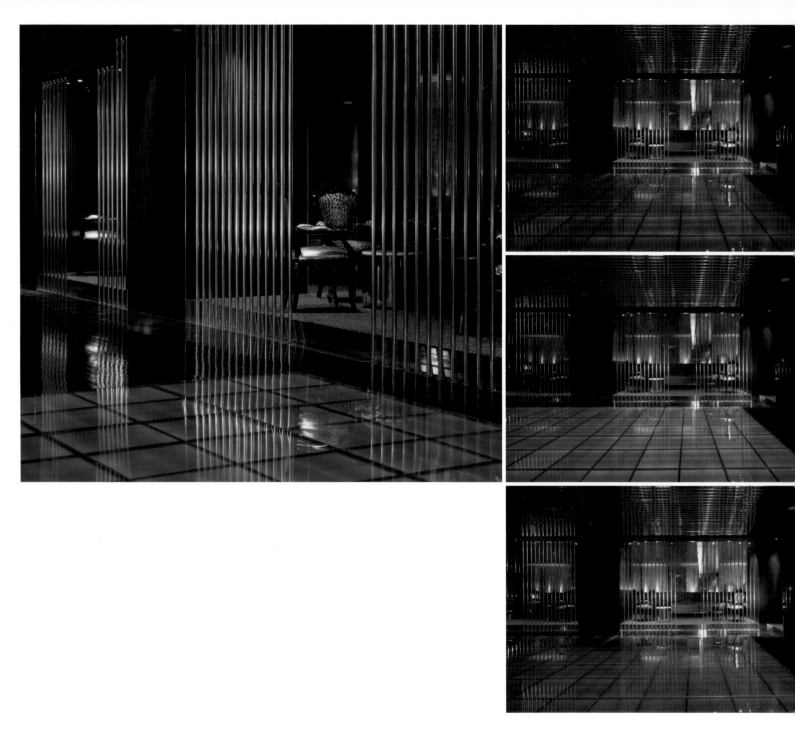

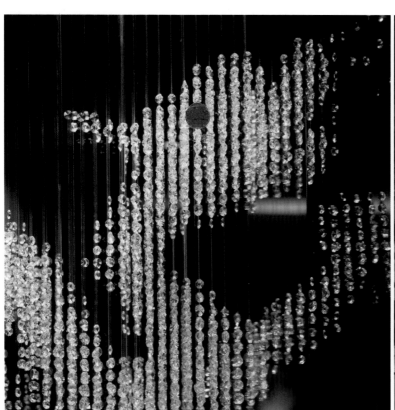

DIX DESIGN ARCHITECTURE | MILAN, ITALY

Website   www.seandix.com
Project   Moschino Cheap & Chic
Location   Milan, Italy
Year of completion 2002
Photo credits   Ramak Fazel

Cheap & Chic is housed on the first floor of the two floor Moschino shop in Milan. The design is based on the juxtaposition of the old and the new, of baroque and minimalism. As a reference to fashion, the Dix studio has used materials related to architecture to recreate fabrics and wefts in the design of the space. Thus, the shape formed by the maple wood emulates the softness of silk and the marble tiles recreate a wavy and flowing material. The display tables are polished stainless steel cubes on which photos of old chests of drawers have been printed and the floor is made of broken pieces of marble which have been carefully fashioned into an attractive mosaic.

Cheap & Chic befindet sich auf der ersten Etage des zweistöckigen Geschäfts von Moschino in Mailand. Bei der Gestaltung dieser Räume hat man das Alte dem Neuen und den Barock dem Minimalismus gegenübergestellt. Als eine Art augenzwinkernde Reminiszenz an die Mode hat das Studio Dix Materialien für die Innenarchitektur verwendet, die Gewebe und Stoffen nachempfunden sind. So wirkt die Struktur des Ahornholzes wie Seidenmoiré und die Marmorkacheln wie ein breiter, gewellter Stoff. Die Ausstellungstische sind mit poliertem Edelstahl bedeckt, auf den man Fotos alter Kommoden aufgedruckt hat, und der Fußboden besteht aus zerbrochenen Marmorstücken, die sorgfältig zu einem schönen Mosaik zusammengesetzt wurden.

Cheap & Chic se encuentra en el primer piso de la tienda de dos plantas de Moschino en Milán. Para el diseño de este espacio se ha recurrido a la yuxtaposición de elementos antiguos y nuevos, barrocos y minimalistas. En un guiño a la moda, el estudio Dix ha resuelto usar materiales relacionados con la arquitectura para recrear tejidos o tramas en el diseño del espacio. Así, el dibujo que forma la madera de arce emula el muaré de la seda y las baldosas de mármol remedan una tela amplia y ondulada. Las mesas expositoras son cubos de acero inoxidable pulido sobre las que se han impreso fotos de antiguas cómodas y para el suelo se ha optado por trozos de mármol roto que se han encajado cuidadosamente como un mosaico atractivo.

Cheap & Chic se trouve au premier de la boutique de deux étages de Moschino à Milan. Dans la conception de cet espace, on a juxtaposé l'ancien et le nouveau, le baroque et le minimalisme. Lançant un clin d'œil à la mode, le studio Dix a utilisé des matériaux liés à l'architecture pour recréer des tissus ou des trames dans le design de l'espace. C'est ainsi que le dessin formé par le bois d'érable imite le moiré de la soie, et les dalles de marbre, un tissu ample et ondulé. Les tables d'exposition sont des cubes d'acier inoxydable poli sur lesquels on a imprimé des photos d'anciennes commodes. Pour le sol, on a opté pour des morceaux de marbre cassé, minutieusement encastrés, à l'instar d'une belle mosaïque.

Lo spazio Cheap & Chic si trova al primo piano della rinnovata boutique a due piani di Via della Spiga a Milano, ed è dedicato alla linea giovane della casa Moschino. L'arredamento interno di questo locale nasce da una giustapposizione di elementi antichi, moderni, minimalisti e barocchi. Strizzando un po' l'occhio alla moda, lo studio Sean Dix, incaricato dell'allestimento, ha selezionato dei materiali adatti a trasferire forme, trame e texture sul piano spaziale. Non a caso, quindi, la forma del legno di acero emula l'effetto moiré della seta e le piastrelle di marmo quello di una stoffa ampia ed ondulata. Gli espositori sono cubi in acciaio inossidabile levigato su cui sono state stampate foto di antichi comò e per terra un attraente mosaico fatto di pezzi di marmo rotto, accuratamente incastrati tra loro.

FABIO NOVEMBRE | MILAN, ITALY

Website	www.novembre.it
Project	Una Hotel Vittoria
Location	Florence, Italy
Year of completion	2003
Photo credits	Fabio Novembre

A whirlwind floral mosaic decorates the entrance to the hotel. Waves are also apparent in the bar and form an unusual rendezvous among its arches as never ending seating. The long corridors of this hotel have been converted into art galleries where large portratis decorate the walls with striking golden frames. The neon lights which adorn various rooms are an original reinterpretation of the classic chandeliers. Finally the rooms reveal an innovative design concept where the walls themselves form almost the only decoration, covered with red square panels through which sparkles of light shine. In the bathroom a baroque style subtle pattern on a green background achieves an attractive effect.

Der Eingangsbereich des Hotels wirkt wie ein fesselnder, mit Blumenmosaik verkleideter Wirbelwind. Die Wellen wiederholen sich in der Bar, wo sie unendlich viele Sitze schaffen und zwischen den Bögen einen Treffpunkt entstehen lassen. Die langen Flure des Hotels werden zu Kunstgalerien, in denen große Gemälde in auffallenden goldenen Rahmen gezeigt werden. Die Neonlampen, die in mehreren Räumen zu finden sind, sind eine originelle Neuinterpretation der klassischen Kronleuchter. Schließlich setzte man auch in den Räumen ein innovatives Gestaltungskonzept um. Hier sind die mit quadratischen, roten Platten verkleideten Wände, in deren Fugen Lichter aufblitzen, fast das einzige Dekorationselement. Das Badezimmer ist mit einer grünen Tapete versehen, dessen subtiles Motiv im barocken Stil einen schönen Effekt erzeugt.

Un torbellino absorbente revestido de mosaico floral es el acceso al hotel. Las ondas se repiten en el bar y logran crear un lugar de encuentro entre sus arcos, a modo de asientos interminables. Los largos pasillos de este hotel se convierten en eventuales galerías de arte para grandes retratos con llamativos marcos dorados. Las lámparas de neón, que se repiten en varias estancias, son una reinterpretación original de los clásicos *chandeliers*. Finalmente, las estancias revelan un concepto de diseño innovador, en el que las mismas paredes son casi la única decoración, revestidas con paneles cuadrados de color rojo y de entre cuyas rendijas asoman destellos de luz. En el baño, un estampado sutil de inspiración barroca sobre verde consigue un atractivo efecto.

Un tourbillon exclusif revêtu de mosaïque florale configure l'accès à l'hôtel. Les ondes se répètent dans le bar, permettant de créer un lieu de rencontre sous ses arches, à l'instar de sièges infinis. Les longs couloirs de cet hôtel se métamorphosent en d'éventuelles galeries d'art pour des grands portraits aux encadrements dorés tape-à-l'œil. Les lampes au néon se retrouvent dans plusieurs pièces, réinterprétant avec originalité les lustres classiques. Finalement, les pièces révèlent un concept de design innovateur où les murs mêmes, avec leur revêtement de panneaux carrés rouges, entre lesquels des fentes renvoient des éclats de lumière, sont presque l'unique décoration. Dans la salle de bains, un imprimé subtil d'inspiration baroque sur un fond vert est du plus bel effet.

Un vortice assorbente rivestito di mosaico floreale costituisce l'accesso all'hotel. Le onde si ripetono nel bar e riescono a creare un luogo di incontro tra i suoi archi, a mo' di sedute interminabili. I lunghi corridoi di questo albergo si trasformano in probabili gallerie d'arte per grandi ritratti con vistose cornici dorate. Le lampade al neon, presenti in diverse stanze, sono un'originale reinterpretazione dei classici *chandelier*. Nel complesso i vari ambienti rivelano un concetto di design innovativo, dove le pareti sono quasi l'unico elemento decorativo. Queste sono rivestite con pannelli quadrati di colore rosso e tra le fessure spuntano riflessi di luce. Nelle pareti del bagno, un leggero stampato di ispirazione barocca su fondo verde crea un effetto accattivante.

FANTASTIC DESIGN WORKS | TOKYO, JAPAN

Website	www.f-fantastic.com
Project	Avalon
Location	Tokyo, Japan
Year of completion	2003
Photo credits	Masaya Yoshimura

The combination of light and darkness are the main players in this space, inspired by a mix of new baroque and art deco, which can be glimpsed beneath the faint lighting. A spectacular chandelier shares the scene with a large disco ball in a curious contrast of styles and eras. Beneath this in clear methacrylate, are the tables of the main space, whose round forms reflect the scarce light. Around this are capitone sofas and seats in striking colors, which in turn contrast with the black floor and ceiling. The latter includes a false level equipped with moldings. This ensemble achieves an elegant and intimate atmosphere.

Das prägendste Element in diesem Lokal ist das Spiel mit Licht und Dunkelheit, inspiriert von einer Mischung aus neuem Barock und Art Déco unter einer sanften Beleuchtung. Ein prachtvoller Kronleuchter teilt sich den Raum mit einer großen Diskokugel, ein interessanter Kontrast von Stilen und Epochen. Darunter befinden sich die Tische in runden Formen aus farblosem Metacrylat in denen sich das wenige Licht reflektiert. Sie sind von Sofas und Sesseln mit gesteppten Postern in auffallenden Farben umgeben, die wiederum einen Kontrast zu dem schwarzen Boden und der schwarzen Decke bilden. An der Decke schuf man mit Leisten den Effekt einer zweiten Ebene. Ein elegantes Lokal mit intimer Atmosphäre.

Los juegos de luz y oscuridad son los auténticos protagonistas en este local, inspirado en una mezcla de nuevo barroco y art déco que se deja vislumbrar bajo la tenue iluminación. Un espectacular *chandelier* comparte escena con una gran bola de discoteca en un curioso contraste de estilos y épocas. Bajo aquél se ubican, en metacrilato incoloro, las mesas del espacio principal que en sus formas redondeadas reflejan la escasa luz. Alrededor se encuentran sofás y butacas en capitoné y colores llamativos, que contrastan a su vez con el suelo y el techo en negro, este último con un falso nivel provisto de molduras. Este conjunto logra una atmósfera elegante e íntima.

Les jeux d'ombre et de lumière sont les vrais protagonistes de cet établissement qui s'inspirent d'un mélange de Nouveau Baroque et d'Art Déco que l'on devine sous le faible éclairage. Un lustre spectaculaire partage la scène avec une grande boule de discothèque dans un contraste insolite de styles et d'époques. En dessous, on découvre, réalisées dans un méthacrylique incolore, les tables de l'espace principal dont les formes rondes reflètent la faible lumière. Tout autour, s'articulent les canapés et fauteuils capitonnés, aux couleurs acidulées, qui contrastent à leur tour avec le sol et le plafond noir, doté d'un faux niveau décoré de moulures. Cet ensemble offre une atmosphère élégante et intime.

I giochi di luce ed oscurità sono i veri protagonisti in questo locale di Tokio, inspirato a una mescolanza di nuovo barocco ed art déco che si lascia intravedere sotto la tenue illuminazione. Uno spettacolare *chandelier* divide la scena con una grande palla da discoteca in un curioso contrasto di stili ed epoche. Sotto il candeliere trovano posto i tavoli in metacrilato incolore dello spazio principale che riflettono la poca luce nelle loro forme arrotondate. Tutto attorno vi sono divani e poltrone in capitonnè e colori sgargianti, in contrasto a loro volta con il pavimento e il soffitto di colore nero, quest'ultimo con un falso livello provvisto di modanature. Tutto questo insieme crea un ambiente intimo ed elegante.

FÉLIX GORDILLO (ARCHITECTURE)/
JOSÉ MARÍA FERNÁNDEZ MAYO (INTERIORS) | LUARCA, OVIEDO, SPAIN

Project   Hotel M
Location   Oviedo, Spain
Year of Completion 2004
Photo credits   Luis Hevia

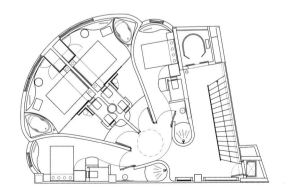

White characterizes the decoration of this hotel, located right in the center of Oviedo and projected by architect Félix Gordillo. Materials like marble and wood create a refined and light space, where the furniture becomes the most important feature. Designer furniture from Philippe Starck, Mies van der Rohe, Hoffman or Vitra — among other well-known names — combine with decorative pieces like Venetian mirrors, Roman bronze pieces and Louis XV, Louis XVI and Napoleon III style furniture. This amalgamation in the decoration achieves a modern and attractive space, to which pieces created by interior designer and decorator José María Fernández Mayo have been added.

Die Dekoration dieses Hotels mitten im Zentrum von Oviedo, das von dem Architekten Félix Gordillo geplant wurde, wird von der Farbe Weiß bestimmt. Materialien wie Marmor und Holz ließen einen Raum mit reinen, klaren Linien entstehen, in dem die Möbel die eigentlichen Hauptdarsteller sind. Designerstücke von Philippe Starck, Mies van der Rohe, Hoffman, Vitra und anderen wurden mit Dekorationselementen wie venezianischen Spiegeln, römischen Bronzen und Möbeln im Stil von Louis XV, Louis XVI und Napoleon III kombiniert. Durch diese dekorative Mischung entstand ein attraktiver und moderner Raum, der durch Objekte des Raumgestalters und Dekorateurs José María Fernández Mayo vervollständigt wurde.

El color blanco caracteriza la decoración de este hotel, situado en pleno centro de Oviedo y proyectado por el arquitecto Félix Gordillo. Los materiales como el mármol y la madera crean un espacio depurado y luminoso, donde el mobiliario adquiere verdadero protagonismo. Muebles de diseño de Philippe Starck, Mies van der Rohe, Hoffman o Vitra —entre otros nombres conocidos— son combinados con piezas de decoración tales como espejos venecianos, bronces romanos y mobiliario de estilo Luis XV, Luis XVI y Napoleón III. Esta amalgama en la decoración logra un espacio moderno y atractivo, al que se le suman piezas creadas por el interiorista y decorador José María Fernández Mayo.

Le blanc définit la décoration de cet hôtel, situé en plein cœur d'Oviedo et conçu par l'architecte Félix Gordillo. Les matériaux comme le marbre et le bois créent un espace épuré et lumineux où le mobilier en devient le véritable protagoniste. Meubles de design de Philippe Starck, Mies van der Rohe, Hoffman ou Vitra —parmi d'autres noms connus— sont combinés à des pièces de décoration tels que miroirs vénitiens, bronzes romains et mobilier de style Louis XV, Louis XVI et Napoléon III. Cet amalgame d'objets de décoration crée un espace moderne et attrayant, auquel s'ajoutent des pièces signées José María Fernández Mayo, architecte d'intérieur et décorateur.

Il colore bianco caratterizza la decorazione di questo hotel, situato in pieno centro a Oviedo e progettato dall'architetto Féliz Gordillo. I materiali come il marmo e il legno creano uno spazio sobrio e luminoso, dove l'arredamento acquista il vero protagonismo. Mobili disegnati da Philippe Starck, Mies van der Rohe, Hoffman o Vitra —tra i nomi più noti— vengono abbinati ad elementi decorativi come specchi veneziani, bronzi romani e pezzi di arredo in stile Luigi XV, Luigi XVI e Napoleone III. Questo amalgama decorativo forma uno spazio moderno e attraente, a cui si aggiungono altri pezzi creati dal designer e arredatore José María Fernández Mayo.

FÉLIX GORDILLO (ARCHITECTURE)/
JOSÉ MARÍA FERNÁNDEZ MAYO (INTERIORS) | LUARCA, OVIEDO, SPAIN

Project   Libretto Hotel
Location   Oviedo, Spain
Year of Completion 2004
Photo credits   Luis Hevia

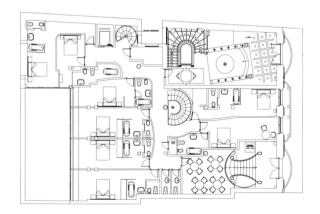

The harmony of styles and materials translate into true music in this hotel, beautifully shown by the pentagram silk screen printed onto the windows of the main lounge. A majestic staircase presides over this space, where white and gold set up a luxurious atmosphere. Here, simple lines with classical touches combine in the benches and tables. The baroque aesthetic has been reinvented in the bedrooms with the use of capitone in the bed headrests. The bathrooms, clad in marble and glass, have been decorated with large black and white photos.

Die Harmonie der Stile und Materialien wird in diesem Hotel zu einer wahren Musikalität. Das bezeugen die im Siebdruckverfahren geschaffenen Notenlinien am Fenster des Hauptsalons. Eine majestätische Treppe beherrscht dieses Gebäude, in dem die Farben Weiß und Gold eine luxuriöse Atmosphäre schaffen. Einfache, klassisch wirkende Linien vermischen sich an den Bänken und Tischen. In den Räumen erfand man die barocke Ästhetik durch den Einsatz von gesteppten Polstern an den Kopfteilen der Betten neu. Die mit Marmor und Glas verkleideten Badezimmer sind mit großen Schwarzweißfotografien dekoriert.

La armonía de estilos y materiales se traduce en auténtica musicalidad en este hotel, como bien lo atestigua el pentagrama serigrafiado sobre el cristal del salón principal. Una majestuosa escalera preside este espacio, donde los colores blanco y dorado instauran un ambiente lujoso. Aquí, líneas simples con toques clásicos se mezclan en bancos y mesas. En las habitaciones se ha reinventado la estética barroca con el uso del capitoné en el cabezal de las camas. Los cuartos de baño, revestidos de mármol y cristal, están decorados con grandes fotografías en blanco y negro.

Dans cet hôtel, l'harmonie entre styles et matières se traduit par une véritable musicalité, comme le témoigne la portée gravée sur la vitre du salon principal. Un majestueux escalier domine cet espace où le blanc et le doré instaurent une atmosphère luxueuse. Ici, des lignes simples aux touches classiques se mêlent aux bancs et tables. Dans les chambres, l'esthétique baroque renaît grâce au tissu capitonné de têtes de lit. Les salles de bains, revêtues de marbre et de verre, sont décorées de grandes photographies en noir et blanc.

L'armonia di stili e materiali si traduce in autentica musicalità in questo hotel, come lo dimostra il pentagramma serigrafato sul vetro del salone principale. Una maestosa scala presiede questo spazio, dove i colori bianco e dorato danno vita a un ambiente lussuoso. Qui, linee semplici dai tocchi classici si mescolano in panche e tavoli. Nelle camere alcuni elementi sono stati rivisitati in chiave barocca come la testata del letto tappezzata in capitonnè. La sale da bagno, rivestite di marmo e cristallo, sono decorate con grandi fotografie in bianco e nero.

GREEK/JOSEP MARIA FONT | BARCELONA, SPAIN

Website	www.greekbcn.com
Project	Tot-hom
Location	Barcelona, Spain
Year of completio	2006
Photo credits	Nuria Vila

The high ceilings and open diaphanous spaces of this shop allow the few decorative pieces to really stand out. The walls are interestingly decorated with laquered black areas and the color white. This combination, together with the sparse furniture and decorative elements, such as the marble fireplace, the classic armchairs, the mirrors and the spectacular chandelier achieve a minimalist baroque ambience. Splashes of red complete the decoration, which also incorporates gold and silver, where each detail has been carefully positioned so that the elegance of the dresses and clothes extends throughout the space.

Die hohen Decken und die weiten, transparent wirkenden Räume dieses Geschäfts machen die wenigen Dekorationselemente zu absoluten Hauptdarstellern. An den Wänden wurde mit Weiß und einigen schwarz lackierten Verkleidungen gespielt. Diese Kombination und die wenigen Möbel und Dekorationselemente – der Marmorkamin, die klassischen Sessel, die Spiegel und der auffallende Kronleuchter – schaffen eine minimalistische und zugleich barocke Atmosphäre. Die Farbe Rot belebt diese Gestaltung, in der auch Silber und Gold zu finden sind und in der jedes Detail sorgfältig ausgewählt wurde, so dass sich die Eleganz der Kleidungsstücke auf den ganzen Raum überträgt.

Los altos techos y los amplios espacios diáfanos de esta tienda permiten que las escasas piezas decorativas logren ser protagonistas absolutas. En las paredes se sucede un juego entre el color blanco y algunos revestimientos en negro con acabado lacado. Esta combinación, junto con el escaso mobiliario y elementos decorativos como la chimena de mármol, las butacas clásicas, los espejos o el espectacular chandelier, logra un ambiente de minimalismo barroco. El rojo pone la nota de color a este diseño, que incluye también el plata y el dorado, y en el que cada detalle se ha colocado minuciosamente de modo que la elegancia de los vestidos y las prendas se ha extendido a todo el espacio.

Les hauts plafonds et les larges espaces diaphanes de cette boutique permettent aux objets de décoration d'en être les seuls protagonistes. Sur les murs, c'est une succession de jeux de couleurs entre le blanc et certains revêtements noirs aux finitions laquées. Cette combinaison de teintes, agrémentée d'un mobilier réduit et d'éléments décoratifs à l'instar de la cheminée en marbre, des fauteuils classiques, des miroirs ou du spectaculaire lustre, crée une ambiance de minimalisme baroque. Le rouge donne le ton du design qui affiche également l'argent et le doré, et dans lequel chaque détail a été minutieusement placé afin que l'élégance des robes et des habits imprègne l'espace entier.

I soffitti alti e gli ampi spazi diafani di questo negozio concedono un protagonismo assoluto ai pochi elementi decorativi. Alle pareti si susseguono un alternarsi tra il bianco e alcuni rivestimenti in nero con finitura laccata. Questo abbinamento, assieme ad accessori come gli specchi, le poltrone e mobili in stile classico, il camino in marmo, o lo spettacolare chandelier, riesce a creare un ambiente barocco-minimalista. Tra i colori usati per gli interni, l'oro e l'argento, su cui spicca un vivace rosso. Elegante e accurato anche il modo in cui i capi d'abbigliamento sono disposti e messi in mostra nei vari spazi della boutique.

GREG NATALE DESIGN | SURRY HILLS NSW, AUSTRALIA

Website	www.gregnatale.com
Project	Cioilino House
Location	Sydney, Australia
Year of Completion	2007
Photo credits	Anson Smart

This project is the result of the renovation of a family residence that dates back to 1940. The intention was to maintain its original style with the aim of creating a small and luxurious home. The decorative scheme uses colors from a painting by Susan O'Doherthy: green, orange, beige, yellow and black. These colors are the inspiration of each and every one of the designs in the rooms of the house. The preservation of some of the original elements helps to create a contemporary and functional version of the previous house. To do this, classical and traditional items of furniture have been combined with iconic design pieces from the 21st century.

Dieses neu gestaltete Wohnhaus entstand durch die Renovierung eines Einfamilienhauses aus dem Jahr 1940. Bei den Arbeiten bemühte man sich darum, den ursprünglichen Stil beizubehalten, und so entstand dieses kleine, luxuriöse Gebäude. Die Farben der Dekoration sind durch ein Gemälde der Autorin Susan O'Doherthy inspiriert, in dem Grün, Orange, Beige, Gelb und Schwarz dominieren. Diese Farben prägen das gesamte Haus und alle einzelnen Räume. Einige der ursprünglichen Elemente blieben erhalten, so dass eine zeitgemäße und originelle Version des vorherigen Wohnhauses entstand. Diese kombinierte man mit klassischen, traditionellen Möbeln und Werken der großen Designer des 21. Jh.

Este proyecto es el resultado de la renovación de una casa familiar que data de 1940. Se ha intentado mantener su estilo original con el fin de lograr una pequeña y lujosa vivienda. El esquema decorativo parte de los colores de una pintura de Susan O'Doherthy: verde, naranja, beige, amarillo y negro. Estos colores han inspirado todos y cada uno de los diseños propios de las estancias de la casa. Se han mantenido algunos elementos originales, de modo que se consigue una versión contemporánea y funcional de la anterior vivienda. Para ello se ha mezclado mobiliario clásico y tradicional con piezas de grandes iconos del diseño del siglo XXI.

Ce projet, fruit de la rénovation d'une maison familiale datant de 1940, a essayé de conserver le style original afin d'obtenir une petite habitation luxueuse. La décoration suit un schéma qui part des tons vert, orange, beige, jaune et noir, tirés d'une peinture signée Susan O'Doherthy. Le design de chacune des pièces de la maison s'inspire de cette gamme chromatique. Les quelques éléments d'origine conservés permettent de réaliser une version contemporaine et fonctionnelle de l'habitation antérieure, dans un mélange de mobilier classique et traditionnel et de pièces portant la signature de grandes icônes du design du XXIe siècle.

Questo progetto è il risultato dell'ammodernamento di una casa familiare che risale al 1940. Si è cercato di mantenere il suo stile originario al fine di creare un'abitazione piccola e lussuosa. Lo schema decorativo parte dai colori di un dipinto di Susan O'Doherthy: verde, arancione, beige, giallo e nero. Questi colori hanno ispirato l'arredamento di ognuna delle stanze della casa. Alcuni elementi originali sono stati mantenuti, ottenendo così una versione contemporanea e funzionale dell'abitazione precedente. A tal fine si sono mescolati mobili in stile classico e tradizionale con singolari pezzi di design realizzati da rinomati artisti del XXI secolo.

GREG NATALE DESIGN | SURRY HILLS NSW, AUSTRALIA

Website	www.gregnatale.com
Project	Superwoman
Location	Sydney, Australia
Year of Completion	2007
Photo credits	Sharrin Reece

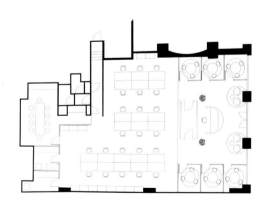

Superwoman is a financial institution with a significant female presence. It was for this reason that the designers here decided to experiment with new colors and forms that are not usually seen in these types of interiors. The innovative floral designs of Tord Bontje play a significant role in the decorative scheme of these offices, which make use of a color palette based on red, black and white; colors that create an environment which is both welcoming and attractive, and relaxing and original. Large windows allow natural light to enter the meeting rooms, which are separated by way of glass walls. These in turn allow the other work areas to benefit from the same light.

Superwoman ist ein Kreditinstitut von Frauen für Frauen. Deshalb entschieden die Innenarchitekten, mit neuen Farben und Formen zu experimentieren, die normalerweise in Räumen solcher Art nicht zu finden sind. Die innovativen Blumenmotive von Tord Bontje spielen eine wichtige Rolle bei der Gestaltung der Büroräume, die auf den Farben Rot, Schwarz und Weiß basiert. Diese lassen eine einladende und anziehende Atmosphäre entstehen, die gleichzeitig entspannend und originell wirkt. Durch die großen Fenster fällt Tageslicht in die Besprechungszimmer, die durch Glas abgetrennt sind, so dass das Licht auch die anderen Arbeitszonen erreicht.

Superwoman es una institución financiera que cuenta con una gran presencia femenina. Por este motivo se decidió experimentar con nuevos colores y formas que no acostumbran a verse en este tipo de interiores. Los innovadores diseños florales de Tord Bontje tienen un papel destacado en el esquema decorativo de estas oficinas, en las que se ha utilizado una paleta cromática basada en el rojo, el negro y el blanco, colores que crean una atmósfera acogedora y atractiva, a la vez que muy relajante y original. Los grandes ventanales permiten la entrada de luz natural hacia las salas de reuniones, que están separadas mediante cristales que permiten así aprovechar esta entrada de luz en las otras áreas de trabajo.

Superwoman est une institution financière dotée d'une forte présence féminine. C'est ce qui explique l'emploi de nouvelles couleurs et formes, plutôt inhabituelles dans ce genre d'intérieurs. D'inspiration florale, les designs innovateurs de Tord Bontjen jouent un rôle primordial dans la conception du décor de ces bureaux où la gamme chromatique, basée sur le rouge, blanc et noir, crée une atmosphère accueillante et séduisante, à la fois très relaxante et originale. Les grandes baies vitrées inondent de lumière naturelle les salles de réunions et, les vitres qui les séparent, lui permettent de fluctuer vers les autres aires de travail.

Superwoman è un'istituzione finanziaria che conta una grande presenza femminile. Per questo motivo si è deciso di sperimentare con nuovi colori e forme che raramente si vedono in questo tipo di interni. Gli innovativi disegni floreali di Tord Bontje hanno un ruolo di rilievo nello schema decorativo di questi uffici, in cui si è adoperata una palette cromatica basata sul rosso, nero e bianco, colori che creano un'atmosfera accogliente e attraente, e al contempo molto rilassante ed originale. Le grandi vetrate consentono l'accesso di abbondante luce naturale nelle sale per riunioni, separate mediante pannelli di vetro, che permettono così di sfruttare la luce anche in altre aree di lavoro.

H K HIA ASSOCIATES | SINGAPORE, SINGAPORE

Project	The Scarlet Hotel
Location	Singapore, Singapore
Year of completion	2004
Photo credits	Grace International Pte. Ltd.

The adjectives "uninhibited" and "different" define the style of The Scarlet to perfection: a boutique hotel strategically located in one of the historic enclaves of Singapore. This daring project preserves the architectural styles and the heritage exemplified by buildings of the city and combines them with a striking design concept which teases the imagination as well as the senses. With a color scheme of red, black and gold, the decoration of the hotel is unique, innovative and with the addition of ostentatious features, gives an attractive overall effect.

Ungehemmt und anders. Diese Adjektive definieren perfekt den Stil von The Scarlet, ein Boutiquehotel, das strategisch günstig in einem der historischen Viertel von Singapur liegt. Bei dieser gewagten Gestaltung bewahrte man den architektonischen Stil der historischen Gebäude der Stadt und ergänzte ihn durch ein auffallendes Designkonzept, das die Phantasie und alle Sinne anregt. Die Dekoration des Hotels, in der die Farben Rot, Schwarz und Gold überwiegen, ist einzigartig und innovativ; sie spielt mit prunkvollen Elementen, um ein attraktives Gesamtbild zu schaffen.

Desinhibido y diferente. Estos adjetivos definen a la perfección el estilo de The Scarlet, un hotel *boutique* situado estratégicamente en uno de los enclaves históricos de Singapur. Esta atrevida apuesta preserva los estilos arquitectónicos de los edificios patrimoniales de la ciudad y los combina con un llamativo concepto de diseño que provoca a la imaginación, así como a todos los sentidos. Con el rojo, el negro y el dorado como paleta principal, la decoración del hotel muestra una estética que pretende ser única e innovadora, y juega con elementos ostentosos para llegar a un atractivo resultado final.

Spontané et différent. Ces adjectifs définissent à merveille le style du Scarlet, un hôtel *boutique* situé à un endroit stratégique, dans une des enclaves historiques de Singapour. Ce pari audacieux conserve les styles architecturaux des édifices du patrimoine de la ville, tout en les combinant à un concept de design intéressant qui éveille à la fois l'imagination et tous les sens. Avec le rouge, le noir et le doré comme palette principale, la décoration de l'hôtel affiche une esthétique qui prétend être unique et innovatrice, tout en jouant avec des éléments somptueux pour parvenir à un ravissant résultat final.

Disinibito e differente. Questi due aggettivi descrivono alla perfezione lo stile di The Scarlet, un hotel boutique situato strategicamente nella storica Eskine Road, a Singapore. La struttura, inaugurata nel 2004, occupa un magnifico edificio art-deco del 1924. Gli arredi, le decorazioni, i materiali e l'illuminazione vengono magistralmente abbinati per trasmettere emozioni forti e piacevoli sensazioni. Con il rosso, il nero e il dorato come palette principale, l'arredamento dell'hotel sfoggia un look decisamente unico ed innovativo che gioca con elementi vistosi per conseguire un accattivante risultato finale.

HECKER PHELAN & GUTHRIE | RICHMOND, VICTORIA, AUSTRALIA

Website	www.hpg.net.au
Project	Comme Bar
Location	Melbourne, Australia
Year of completion	2005
Photo credits	Trevor Mein/Meinphoto

Comme is located in front of the historic Alfred Square in Melbourne. The vinoteca is situated on the ground floor alongside the restaurant Comme Kitchen and is a sensational space with a marble bar top in the centre; chandeliers, a large hand woven rug and luxurious leather ottoman sofas offer a chance to to unwind away from the hustle and bustle of the city. The wine list offers a host of exquisite wines from all over the world. The Grand room and Onyx room are situated on the upper level beyond the staircase and comprise two dynamic spaces which are also decorated in a modern and elegant baroque style. They serve as an ideal location for a cocktail party, meeting, conferences or any other special kind or celebration in an atmosphere brimming with luxury and glamour.

L'espace Comme se situe face à la place historique Alfred de Melbourne. Au rez-de-chaussée, à côté du restaurant Comme Kitchen, se trouve la vinothèque, un espace extraordinaire juste doté d'un comptoir de bar en marbre, avec des lustres qui descendent du plafond, un grand tapis fait à la main et de luxeux divans ottomans en cuir où se relaxer loin de l'agitation de la ville. Sa carte propose une excellente sélection de vins exquis venus du monde entier. Au-delà des escaliers, le niveau supérieur accueille la Onyx Room et le Grand Room, deux espaces polyvalents, également décorés dans un style baroque élégant et moderne, offrant ainsi un lieu idéal pour organiser cocktails, réunions, conférences et tout autre évènement dans une ambiance de luxe et glamour.

Vor dem historischen Platz Alfred de Melbourne befindet sich das Comme. Im Erdgeschoss neben dem Restaurant Comme Kitchen ist eine Vinothek untergebracht, ein auffallender Raum mit einer Marmorstange im Zentrum, Kronleuchtern an der Decke, einem großen, handgearbeiteten Teppich und einem luxuriösen ottomanischen Ledersofa, auf dem man sich von der Hektik der Stadt erholen kann. Hier werden erlesene Weine aus der ganzen Welt angeboten. Im Obergeschoss hinter den Treppen liegen der Onyx Room und The Grand Room, zwei flexible Räume, die ebenfalls in einem eleganten und modernen Barockstil dekoriert sind. Sie eignen sich ideal für Cocktailempfänge, Besprechungen, Vorlesungen und andere Arten von Veranstaltungen in einer luxuriösen und glamourösen Atmosphäre.

Di fronte alla storica piazza Alfred di Melbourne si trova lo spazio Comme. Al piano terra, accanto al ristorante Comme Kitchen, si trova l'enoteca, uno spazio sensazionale con al centro un bancone in marmo, chandelier appesi al soffitto, un gran tappeto fatto a mano e lussuosi divani ottomani in pelle dove rilassarsi, lontano dal trambusto della città. La sua eccellente selezione propone squisiti vini di tutto il mondo. Al livello superiore, una volta superate le scale, trovano posto la Onyx Room e The Grand Room, due spazi flessibili anch'essi decorati secondo uno stile barocco elegante e moderno. La cornice ideale dove poter organizzare cocktail, riunioni, conferenze e qualsiasi altra celebrazione, in un'atmosfera piena di lusso e glamour.

Frente a la histórica plaza Alfred de Melbourne se encuentra el espacio Comme. En la planta baja, junto al restaurante Comme Kitchen, se sitúa la vinoteca, un espacio sensacional con una barra de bar de mármol justo en el centro, chandeliers que cuelgan del techo, una gran alfombra hecha a mano y lujosos sofás otomanos de piel donde relajarse lejos del ajetreo de la ciudad. Su excelente selección propone exquisitos vinos de todo el mundo. En el nivel superior, más allá de las escaleras, se extienden la Onyx Room y The Grand Room, dos espacios flexibles también decorados con un estilo barroco elegante y moderno, que proponen un lugar ideal donde organizar cócteles, reuniones, conferencias y cualquier otra celebración en una atmósfera llena de lujo y glamour.

HOSPES DESIGN | BARCELONA, SPAIN

Website	www.hospes.es
	www.designhotels.com
Project	Hospes Palacio de los Patos
Location	Granada, Spain
Year of completion	2006
Photo credits	Hospes Palacio de los Patos

Through careful restoration work this 19th century palace has been converted into The Hospes Palacio de Los Patos Hotel in Granada. The most beautiful and useful parts of the original construction have been conserved in order to give each corner a new function without losing years of history. Every room boasts one element which renders it unique, as for example, a large ceiling rose or the structural remains of what was once a dovecote and, in many, the embossed plasterwork of the ceiling remains. Materials such as wood, marble and stone are in harmony with those of the main structure. The furniture combines a style of pure lines with elements such as wrought iron headrests, large patterned rugs and lamps and bathroom furniture of a more sophisticated nature.

Im Rahmen einer gut geplanten Restaurierung baute man diesen Palast aus dem 19. Jh. in Granada in das Hotel Hospes Palacios de los Patos um. Alles, was an der ursprünglichen Konstruktion schön und nützlich war, blieb erhalten, so dass man jeden Winkel neu nutzte, ohne die langjährige Geschichte zu leugnen. Jeder Raum ist mit einem Element ausgestattet, das ihn einzigartig macht, z. B. eine große Rosette oder das strukturelle Erbe des einstigen Taubenschlags. In vielen Räumen hat man den Deckenstuck erhalten. Materialien wie Holz, Marmor und Stein passen ausgezeichnet zur Hauptstruktur. Auch die Möbel mit ihren reinen Linien und Elemente wie schmiedeeiserne Bettengitter, große bedruckte Teppiche und edle Lampen und Badezimmermöbel fügen sich ästhetisch schön ins Bild.

Tras una cuidada restauración, este palacio del siglo XIX se ha convertido en el hotel Hospes Palacio de los Patos en Granada. De la antigua construcción se conservó todo lo bello y útil, de manera que, sin omitir años y años de historia, se ha dotado a cada rincón de un nuevo uso. Cada estancia posee un elemento que la individualiza, por ejemplo, un gran rosetón o la herencia estructural de lo que fue un antiguo palomar, y en muchas de ellas destacan los relieves enyesados del techo. Los materiales como la madera, el mármol o la piedra armonizan con los de la estructura principal. Lo mismo ocurre con el mobiliario, que combina las líneas depuradas y elementos como cabezales de forja, grandes alfombras estampadas o lámparas y muebles de baño de un diseño más sofisticado.

Après une restauration peaufinée, ce palais du XIXe siècle est devenu l'hôtel Hospes Palacio de los Patos à Grenade. De l'ancienne construction, on a préservé tout ce qui est beau et utile, de sorte que, sans faire fi du passé historique, chaque recoin a reçu une nouvelle fonction. Chaque pièce possède un élément qui la personnalise, à l'instar d'une grande rosace ou de l'héritage structurel d'un ancien pigeonnier et dans de nombreuses pièces les reliefs en plâtre du plafond sont mis en valeur. Les matériaux comme le bois, le marbre ou la pierre s'harmonisent avec ceux de la structure principale. Il en est de même du mobilier, qui conjugue des lignes épurées à des éléments tels les têtes de lit en fer forgé, les grands tapis imprimés ou les lampes et meubles de salle de bains au design plus sophistiqué.

In seguito ad un'accurata ristrutturazione, questo palazzo del XIX sec. si è convertito nell'hotel Hospes Palacio de los Patos, a Granada. I lavori hanno recuperato le parti più belle e quelle ancora utili dell'edificio preesistente, adeguando ogni angolo al rispettivo nuovo uso. Ogni stanza possiede un elemento che la caratterizza. Ad esempio, un grande rosone, la struttura di una ex colombaia, e la presenza in molti soffitti di rilievi in gesso. I materiali come il legno, il marmo o la pietra si trovano in perfetta armonia con quelli della struttura principale. Lo stesso accade con la mobilia, che abbina linee sobrie ed elementi come capezzali in ferro battuto, grandi tappeti con stampati o lampade e mobili da bagno dal design più raffinato.

IAN SCHRAGER COMPANY (OWNER)/
MICHAEL OVERINGTON, ANDA ANDREI (DESIGN) | NEW YORK, UNITED STATES

Project	Gramercy Park Hotel
Location	New York, United States
Year of Completion	2006
Photos credits	Gramercy Park Hotel

The essence of the old Gramercy Park Hotel has remained in tact despite the transformation carried out by owner Ian Schrager and two of his frequent allies: Michael Overington and Anda Andrei. The building stands in front of the park that bears the same name, Gramercy; an island of serenity amidst the hustle and bustle of New York. Its original bohemian style has been rescued in a reinvention that harmonizes with the 21st century. Despite the preservation of its classical line, the decoration includes a very particular combination of styles, with fabulous pieces of furniture and art, as well as an exceptional use of color. The old mixes with the contemporary in a chromatic display where elegance shines through.

L'essence de l'ancien Gramercy Park Hotel a été conservée malgré la transformation réalisée par son propriétaire Ian Schrager et deux de ses fidèles collaborateurs : Michael Overington et Anda Andrei. L'édifice s'élève devant le parc qui lui a donné son nom, Gramercy, véritable havre de paix dans le tourbillon de New York. Son style bohème initial a été sauvegardé dans une réhabilitation en harmonie avec le XXIe siècle. La décoration de cet hôtel comprend, malgré sa ligne classique, une combinaison particulière de styles, avec des pièces de mobilier et d'art fabuleuses, ainsi qu'un emploi exceptionnel des couleurs. L'art séculaire se mélange au contemporain, dans une danse chromatique où l'élégance est clairement de mise.

Es war den Planern gelungen, die Essenz des Gramercy Park Hotel trotz der Umgestaltung, die der Eigentümer Ian Schrager durchführen ließ, zu erhalten. Dies ist Michael Overington und Anda Andrei zu verdanken. Das Gebäude steht vor dem gleichnamigen Park Gramercy, einer Insel der Gelassenheit inmitten der hektischen Stadt New York. Der originale Bohemestil wurde auf so geschickte Art neu erfunden, dass er mit dem 21. Jh. im Einklang steht. Obwohl die klassische Linie beibehalten wurde, stellt die Dekoration des Hotels eine eigenartige Stilmischung mit auffallenden Möbeln und Kunstwerken und einer interessanten, farblichen Gestaltung dar. Jahrhundertealtes verbindet sich mit Neuem, ein bunter Tanz voller Eleganz.

L'essenza originale dell'antico Gramercy Park Hotel è stata mantenuta nonostante la trasformazione portata a termine dal proprietario Ian Schrager e da due dei suoi fedeli alleati: Michael Overington e Anda Andrei. L'edificio si erge davanti al parco da cui prende il nome, Gramercy, un'oasi di serenità in mezzo al trambusto di New York. Il suo stile bohémien autentico è stato ricreato e messo in armonia con un'ambientazione più consona al XXI sec. Nonostante la linea classica mantenuta, l'arredamento include una particolare combinazione di stili, con favolosi oggetti d'arte, così come un uso eccezionale del colore. Il classico si mescola al contemporaneo, in un ballo cromatico dove a farla da padrona è l'eleganza.

La esencia del antiguo Gramercy Park Hotel se ha logrado mantener a pesar de la transformación llevada a cabo por el propietario Ian Schrager y dos de sus habituales aliados: Michael Overington y Anda Andrei. El edificio se erige ante el parque del que recibe su nombre, Gramercy, una isla de serenidad en la convulsa Nueva York. Su estilo bohemio original ha sabido rescatarse en una reinvención que armoniza con el siglo XXI. Su decoración incluye, pese a la línea clásica mantenida, una particular combinación de estilos, con fabulosas piezas de mobiliario y de arte, así como un uso excepcional del color. Lo centenario se mezcla con lo contemporáneo, en un baile cromático donde la elegancia se hace evidente.

JOI DESIGN INNENARCHITEKTEN | HAMBURG, GERMANY

Website	www.joi-design.com
Project	Minibar Hannover
Location	Hannover, Germany
Year of completion	2006
Photo credits	Joi Design

The Minibar, housed in the City Hotel am Thieleplatz in Hanover serves as a café during the day and a cocktail bar at night. The high ceilings are painted deep red which is also the color of the upholstered capitone sofas with endless backrests. This strong color contrasts sharply with the black and white floral patterened wall paper, which even covers part of the ceiling. The impressive chandeliers hanging above the sofas, which have been modernized with screens — in keeping with the rest of the bar — are one of the higligehts of this place. The chromatic range, based on tomato red and coffee brown, is completed by splashes of black and white and also by subtle touches of yellow bringing warmth to the space.

Tagsüber ein Café und nachts eine Cocktailbar. So gestaltete man die Minibar im City Hotel am Thielenplatz in Hannover. Die hohen Decken wurden in einem intensiven Rot gestrichen, das sich auch an den gepolsterten Sofas und den vielen Rückenlehnen wiederholt. Diese starke Farbe bildet einen Kontrast zu den schwarz-weißen Wänden mit Blumendruck, teilweise sogar an der Decke zu finden. Die auffallendsten Elemente sind die großen Kronleuchter, die über den Sofas hängen und mit Schirmen bedeckt wurden, so dass sie moderner wirken und besser ins Bild passen. Die Farbpalette, die auf Tomatenrot und Kaffeebraun basiert, wird mit schwarz-weißen Elementen und etwas Gelb kombiniert, das den Raum wärmer wirken lässt.

Café durante el día y *cocktail-bar* durante la noche. Ésta es la propuesta del Minibar, situado en el City Hotel am Thielenplatz en Hanover. Los altos techos están pintados de un rojo intenso que se repite también en los sofás de tapizado capitoné e interminables respaldos. Este fuerte color contrasta con el papel de las paredes, en blanco y negro con estampados florales, que incluso llega a cubrir parte del techo. Una de las piezas que más destacan son los grandes *chandeliers* que cuelgan del techo a lo largo de toda la zona de los sofás y que se han cubierto con pantallas para dotarlos de un aspecto mucho más moderno, en consonancia con el local. La gama cromática, basada en el rojo tomate y el marrón café, se completa con las notas de blanco y negro y también con los sutiles toques de amarillo que aportan calidez al espacio.

Café pendant la journée et *cocktail bar* durant la nuit. C'est ce que propose le Minibar, situé dans le City Hotel de la Thielenplatz à Hanovre. Les hauts plafonds sont peints d'un rouge intense qui se répète sur les divans et dossiers capitonnés interminables. Cette couleur forte contraste avec le papier des murs, en noir et blanc aux imprimés fleuris qui recouvrent même une partie du plafond. Parmi les éléments les plus remarquables citons les grands lustres qui descendent du plafond le long de toute la zone des divans et qui, entourés d'abat-jour, revêtent une allure beaucoup plus moderne, en harmonie avec l'établissement. La gamme chromatique, basée sur le rouge tomate et le marron café, s'agrémente de pointes de noir et blanc conjuguées à de subtiles touches de jaune qui rendent l'espace chaleureux.

Caffè di giorno e *cocktail-bar* di sera. Questa è la proposta del Minibar, situato all'interno del City Hotel am Thielenplatz di Hannover. Gli alti soffitti sono dipinti di un rosso intenso che si ripete anche nei divani con imbottitura capitonné e interminabili schienali. Questo colore acceso contrasta con la carta da parati, in bianco e nero con motivi floreali, che arriva a coprire persino parte del soffitto. Tra gli elementi di arredo che spiccano di più, i grandi *chandelier* che pendono dal soffitto, disposti lungo tutta la zona dei divani e ricoperti con paralumi per dotarli di un aspetto molto più moderno, in consonanza con il locale. La gamma cromatica, basata sul rosso pomodoro e il marrone caffè, si completa con le note di bianco e nero ed anche con i leggeri tocchi di giallo che apportano calore allo spazio.

KWID/KELLY WEARSTLER | LOS ANGELES, UNITED STATES

Website	www.kwid.com
Project	Body English
Location	Las Vegas, United States
Year of completion	2003
Photo credits	KWID

Body English is a newly renovated night club in the Hard Rock Hotel-Casino. The designer Kelly Wearstler has created an extremely luxurious and exclusive ambience. Walls made entirely of mirrors or covered in black with Baccarat glass chandeliers, and leather benches and sofas achieve an atmosphere worthy of its setting and new name. A bar, an area of sofas of a more intimate ambience and the VIP zone are all located on the upper level. Downstairs there is another area of sofas from where to observe the dance floor, over which hangs a large lamp which changes color as the night unfolds. The bathroom is as elegant or more so than the rest of Body English, with gold swan taps and a large mirror illuminated with candelabras.

Das Body English ist der vor kurzem renovierte Nachtclub des Hard Rock Hotel-Casino. Die Designerin Kelly Wearstler hat das Lokal höchst luxuriös und exklusiv gestaltet. Verspiegelte oder schwarz verkleidete Wände, Kronleuchter aus Baccaratkristall, Lederbänke und Sofas schaffen eine Umgebung, die ihrer Lage und ihres Prestiges würdig ist. Im Obergeschoss befinden sich die Bar, eine private, mit Sofas ausgestattete Zone und die VIP-Lounge. Unten gibt es einen weiteren Bereich mit Sofas, von dem aus man die Tanzfläche beobachten kann, überragt von einer großen Lampe, die im Laufe der Nacht ihre Farbe verändert. Das Bad ist noch eleganter als alles andere im Body English, die Armaturen sind goldene Schwäne, und es gibt einen großen, von Kandelabern beleuchteten Spiegel.

El Body English es el club nocturno recientemente renovado del Hard Rock Hotel-Casino. La diseñadora Kelly Wearstler ha dotado a este local de un lujo y una exclusividad llevadas hasta su máxima expresión. Paredes de espejo o revestidas en negro, *chandeliers* de cristal de Baccarat y bancos y sofás de piel logran crear un ambiente digno de su renombre y ubicación. En el piso superior se encuentra un bar, un área de sofás de ambiente más íntimo y la zona VIP. Abajo, otra zona de sofás desde la que observar la pista de baile, sobre la que pende una gran lámpara que cambia de color a medida que avanza la noche. El baño es tan elegante o más que el resto del Body English, con cisnes dorados a modo de grifos y un amplio espejo iluminado con candelabros.

Le Body English est la boite de nuit récemment rénovée du Hard Rock Hotel-Casino. La designer Kelly Wearstler a doté ce local d'un luxe et d'une exclusivité portés au comble de leur expression. Murs habillés de miroirs ou revêtus de noir, lustres de cristal de Baccarat, bancs et divans en peau parviennent à créer une ambiance à la hauteur de sa réputation et de son emplacement. L'étage accueille un bar, un espace doté de canapés pour une ambiance plus intime et une zone VIP avec en contrebas, une autre zone de canapés d'où l'on observe la piste de danse, surplombée d'une grande lampe qui change de couleurs au fil de la nuit. La salle de bains est d'une élégance telle qu'elle outrepasse celle du reste du Body English, avec ses robinets en forme de cygnes dorés, et un grand miroir éclairé de chandeliers.

Il Body English è il club notturno, recentemente rinnovato, dell'Hard Rock Hotel-Casino. La designer Kelly Wearstler ha dotato questo locale di un lusso e di un'esclusività portati fino alla loro massima espressione. Pareti a specchio o rivestite di nero, *chandelier* di cristallo Baccarat e panche e divani in pelle riescono a creare un ambiente degno della sua fama e della location. Al piano superiore si trova un bar, un'area con divani più intima e la zona VIP. Sotto, un'altra zona di divani da cui osservare la pista da ballo su cui pende un gran lampadario che col passare delle ore cambia colore. Il bagno è elegante quanto o più del resto del Body English, con rubinetti a forma di cigni dorati e un ampio specchio illuminato mediante candelabri.

KWID/KELLY WEARSTLER | LOS ANGELES, UNITED STATES

Website	www.kwid.com
Project	Viceroy Palm Springs
Location	Palm Springs (CA), United States
Year of completion	2006
Photo credits	Kor Hotel Group

The ornamental borders, which decorate some of the rooms as well as most of the details in the common zones, reveal clearly the Greek influence in the decoration, blended with classic furniture, numerous sophisticated mirrors and a glass teardrop curtain. The palette based on white, black and citric yellow brings elegance and sophistication to the hotel as well as warmth, in harmony with the arid and desert zone in which it is located, at the foot of the San Jacinto mountains and in the heart of Palm Springs, California.

Die Zierstreifen in einigen Räumen und viele der Dekorationselemente in den Gemeinschaftsräumen zeigen die deutlich griechische Prägung der Dekoration in Kombination mit klassischen Möbeln, vielen edlen Spiegeln und einer Gardine aus Glastränen. Die Farbpalette, die auf Weiß, Schwarz und Zitronengelb basiert, lässt das Hotel edel und elegant wirken und schafft eine warme Atmosphäre, die sich im Einklang mit der trockenen, wüstenartigen Region befindet, in der es liegt: in den Bergen von San Jacinto und im Herzen von Palm Springs, Kalifornien.

Las cenefas que se repiten en algunas de las estancias, así como muchos de los detalles decorativos que se encuentran en zonas comunes, revelan la clara inspiración griega de la decoración, mezclada con mobiliario clásico, numerosos espejos sofisticados y una cortina de lágrimas de cristal. La paleta, basada en el blanco, el negro y el amarillo cítrico, aporta elegancia y sofisticación al hotel, además de una calidez que se conjuga con la zona árida y desértica en la que se encuentra, bajo las montañas de San Jacinto y en el corazón de Palm Springs en California.

Les plinthes qui se répètent dans quelques unes des pièces, ainsi que les nombreux détails décoratifs visibles dans les zones communes, révèlent clairement l'inspiration grecque de la décoration à laquelle se mêlent mobilier classique, divers miroirs sophistiqués et un rideau de larmes de verre. La palette de couleurs, basée sur le blanc, le noir et le jaune citron, confère à l'hôtel élégance, sophistication, et, de surcroît, une touche chaleureuse allant de paire avec la zone aride et désertique où il se trouve, au pied des montagnes de San Jacinto et au cœur de Palm Springs en Californie.

Le fasce che si ripetono in alcune stanze, così come i vari dettagli decorativi presenti nelle zone comuni, rivelano una chiara ispirazione greca dell'arredamento dove spiccano mobili classici, pregevoli specchi e una tenda con lacrime di cristallo. La palette cromatica, incentrata sul bianco, nero e giallo, apporta eleganza e raffinatezza all'hotel, rendendo accoglienti e caldi i suoi ambienti, in netto contrasto con la zona arida e deserta dove sorge la struttura, sotto le montagne di San Jacinto, nel cuore di Palm Springs, in California.

LUIS GALLIUSSI | MADRID, SPAIN

Website	www.luisgalliussi.com
Project	Negro de Anglona
Location	Madrid, Spain
Year of completion	2004
Photo credits	Manolo Yllera

This restaurant is housed in the basement of a period Madrid palace, the Palace of Prince of Anglona. This unique setting, characterized by history and sophistication, has lent itself to an interesting creation of modern contrasts with very attractive results. Decorated by the prestigious architect and interior designer Luis Galliussi, el Negro de Anglona is set out behind a majestic entrance. Spectacularly patterned curtains hang from the high ceilings which are adorned with modern chandeliers. This paves the way to the restaurant where black walls and a soft light create an elegant ambience which is highlighted by magnificent images reproducing classic lounges and staircases.

Dieses Restaurant liegt im Erdgeschoss eines alten Palastes in Madrid, dem Palacio del Príncipe de Anglona. Dieser einzigartige, von Geschichte und Noblesse geprägte Rahmen ermöglichte ein Spiel mit modernen Kontrasten, das zu einem sehr gelungenen Ergebnis führte. Durch einen majestätischen Eingang betritt man das Restaurant El Negro de Anglona, das von dem bekannten Architekten und Innenarchitekten Luis Galliussi gestaltet wurde. Luxuriöse, bedruckte Gardinen hängen von hohen Decken herab; der Raum wird mit modernen Kronleuchtern illuminiert. Nach diesem beeindruckenden Entrée gelangt man in das Restaurant selbst, wo edle Gemälde an schwarzen Wänden hängen und sanftes Licht die Freitreppen und klassischen Salons erhellt, um eine elegante Umgebung zu schaffen.

Este restaurante está situado en los bajos de un antiguo palacio madrileño, el Palacio del Príncipe de Anglona. Este marco singular, que se distingue por su historia y sofisticación, ha permitido el juego de contrastes modernos con un resultado atractivo. Decorado por el prestigioso arquitecto e interiorista Luis Galliussi, el Negro de Anglona se resguarda tras una majestuosa entrada. Unas cortinas estampadas espectaculares penden de los altos techos, a su vez decorados con modernos *chandeliers*. Tras este preámbulo, se accede al restaurante, cuyas paredes negras y luz tenue crean un ambiente elegante con imágenes magníficas que reproducen escalinatas y salones clásicos.

Ce restaurant est situé au rez-de-chaussée d'un ancien palais madrilène, le Palacio del Príncipe de Anglona. Ce cadre unique, qui se démarque par son histoire et son élégance, a permis de réaliser un jeu de contrastes modernes donnant un résultat charmant. Décoré par le prestigieux Luis Galliussi, à la fois architecte et architecte d'intérieur, le Negro de Anglona se protège derrière une majestueuse entrée. Des rideaux imprimés spectaculaires descendent des hauts plafonds, décorés à leur tour de lustres modernes. Après ce « préambule », on accède au restaurant dont les murs noirs, dotés d'images magnifiques reproduisant perrons et salons classiques, associés à la lumière tamisée, créent une ambiance tout en élégance.

Questo ristorante occupa il pianterreno di un antico palazzo madrileno, il Palazzo del Principe di Anglona. Questa cornice singolare, ricca di storia ed eleganza, ha permesso un gioco di contrasti moderni, dai risultati davvero attraenti. Arredato dal prestigioso architetto e interior designer Luis Galliussi, il Negro de Anglona cela i suoi ambienti dietro un maestoso ingresso. Spettacolari tende stampate pendono dai soffitti alti, a loro volta decorati da moderni *chandelier*. Oltrepassato questo spazio preliminare, si accede al ristorante, le cui pareti nere e la luce tenue creano un ambiente elegante con immagini magnifiche che riproducono scalinate e saloni classici.

M41LH2 | HELSINKI, FINLAND

Website   www.m41lh2.com
Project   Helsinki Club
Location   Helsinki, Finland
Year of completion 2003
Photo credits   Matti Pyykkö

This project posed a great challenge for the designers given that it entailed the creation of a new image for a well known casino and nightspot which has existed for thirty years on the Helsinki nightscene. Thus the designers searched for ideas and details which would give each space its own unique atmosphere. The lounge, situated on the upper level, is a magnificent example of extravagance where all the walls, the ceiling and the floor are furnished in a Baroque inspired patterned carpet — diverging greatly from the luminosity and bright colors of the rest of the club.

Die Gestaltung dieser Lounge stellte eine große Herausforderung an die Planer dar, denn das Aussehen eines bekannten Nachtclubs und Kasinos, der schon seit dreißig Jahren in Helsinki funktionierte, sollte verändert werden. Man suchte Ideen und Lösungen, um jedem Raum eine einzigartige Atmosphäre zu verleihen. So zeigt sich die Lounge im Obergeschoss als beeindruckend extravagant. Wände, Decke und Boden sind mit einem Teppichboden gepolstert, der mit barock inspirierten Medaillen bedruckt ist. Dieser Stil bildet einen Kontrast zu der Helle und den lebendigen Farben der restlichen Räume.

Este proyecto constituía un gran reto para los diseñadores, ya que se trataba de proyectar una nueva imagen para un conocidísimo local nocturno y casino con más de treinta años de trayectoria en Helsinki. Ante este reto, se buscaron ideas y detalles que otorgasen a cada uno de los espacios una atmósfera única. Así, el *lounge*, situado en el nivel superior, se revela ante los clientes en un magnífico espectáculo de extravagancia, donde todas las paredes, el techo y el suelo están forrados de una moqueta con estampados de medallones inspirados en el arte barroco. Un estilo que contrasta con la luminosidad y los colores vivos del resto del local.

Pour les designers, ce projet représentait un grand défi, puisqu'il s'agissait de concevoir une nouvelle image pour un établissement nocturne et casino très connu à Helsinki, qui existait depuis plus de trente ans. Face à ce défi, les concepteurs se sont mis en quête d'idées et détails pour conférer à chaque espace une atmosphère unique. Ainsi, le *lounge*, situé au niveau supérieur, dévoile aux clients un magnifique spectacle d'extravagance, où les murs, le plafond et le sol sont recouverts d'une moquette imprimée de médaillons inspirés de l'art baroque. Un style qui contraste avec la luminosité et les couleurs vives du reste de l'établissement.

Questo progetto ha significato una grande sfida per i designer, visto che l'obiettivo era dare una nuova immagine ad un noto locale notturno e casinò di Helsinki con oltre trent'anni di storia alle spalle. Pertanto si sono cercati dei particolari e delle idee che concedessero ad ognuno degli spazi un'atmosfera unica. Così, il lounge, situato al livello superiore, si rivela ai clienti in un magnifico spettacolo di stravaganza, dove tutte le pareti, il soffitto e il pavimento sono rivestiti da moquette con stampati che riproducono dei medaglioni ispirati all'arte barocca. Uno stile in contrasto con la luminosità e i colori accesi del resto del locale.

MARCEL WANDERS | AMSTERDAM, THE NETHERLANDS

Website	www.marcelwanders.com
Project	Lute Suites
Location	Amsterdam, The Netherlands
Year of completion	2006
Photo credits	Inga Powilleit, Tatjana Quax, Sebastiaan Westerweel

The renowned Bisazza glass mosaic work is the highlight of many rooms and spaces of this hotel. The mosaics create different patterns in varied chromatic ranges and cover the bathroom walls in some of the suites, for example, the number one and six with designs by Marcel Wanders created exlusively for the Hotel. The rest of the decoration, as much in the bedrooms as in the bathrooms, is based on a blend of sombre and elegant minimalism and small details such as tables and lamps which along with the mosaics bring a neobaroque air to the overall look of the hotel.

Les fameux carreaux de verre de Bisazza sont à l'honneur dans plusieurs chambres et espaces de cet hôtel. Les mosaïques créent des dessins variés dans diverses gammes chromatiques qui recouvrent les murs des salles de bains et de certaines suites, comme les numéros un et six, designs signés Marcel Wanders et créés spécialement pour l'Hôtel Lute. Le reste de la décoration, dans les pièces comme dans les salles des bains, repose sur un mélange entre un minimalisme élégant et sobre et des petits détails comme les tables et les lampes qui, à côté des mosaïques, apportent un air néo baroque à l'esthétique globale de l'hôtel.

Die berühmten Glasmosaiksteinchen von Bisazza schmücken verschiedene Räume dieses Hotels. Die Mosaiken bilden Muster in unterschiedlichen Farben an den Wänden der Bäder In den Suites, so in der Nummer eins und sechs. Sie wurden eigens von Marcel Wanders für das Hotel Lute gestaltet. Die übrige Dekoration der Räume und Bäder basiert auf einer Kombination von elegantem, schlichtem Minimalismus mit kleinen Elementen wie Tischen und Lampen, die im Zusammenspiel mit den Mosaiken der allgemeinen Ästhetik des Hotels einen neobarocken Touch geben.

Le note tessere di vetro di Bisazza costituiscono il principale elemento di richiamo in varie stanze e spazi di questo albergo. I mosaici creano svariati disegni in gamme cromatiche diverse e coprono le pareti dei bagni di alcune suite, come la numero uno e la sei, con disegni dello stesso Marcel Wanders realizzati appositamente per l'Hotel Lute. Il resto dell'arredamento, sia nei bagni che nelle camere, si basa su una combinazione di minimalismo elegante e sobrio e piccoli dettagli quali tavoli e lampade, che assieme ai mosaici, apportano un'aria neobarocca all'estetica globale dell'hotel.

Las famosas teselas de vidrio de Bisazza son el mayor reclamo en varias habitaciones y espacios de este hotel. Los mosaicos crean distintos dibujos en gamas cromáticas variadas que cubren las paredes de los baños de algunas *suites*, como las número uno y seis, con diseños del propio Marcel Wanders creados especialmente para el Hotel Lute. El resto de la decoración, tanto de las estancias como de los baños, está basada en una mezcla entre un minimalismo elegante y sobrio y pequeños detalles como mesas y lámparas que, junto con los mosaicos, aportan un aire neobarroco a la estética global del hotel.

MASOERO & DE CARLO ARCHITETTI ASSOCIATI | MILAN, ITALY

Website	www.mdcarchitetti.it
Project	Palazzo Anguissola da Grazzano
Location	Piacenza, Italia
Year of completion	2005
Photo credits	Duccio Malagamba

In 1770, the architect Cosimo Morelli planned this palace situated in Piacenza. It is a work of art carried out with rigorous precision and is set out around a main courtyard, with porticos on three of its sides and a secondary, gardened courtyard. Its architectural and decorative style responds to elegant late baroque with neoclassic elements and influences. The present owners were somewhat worried that the palace would lose some of its history after the last resoration, but thanks to the meticulous work, the original aesthetic of the construction has been revived, including the exterior façade and the roofs as well as the interior. Furthermore, each new piece has been selected very carefully in order to fully preserve the historic essence of this splendid Italian palace.

En 1770, l'architecte Cosimo Morelli a conçu ce palais situé à Piacenza. Il s'agit d'une œuvre maîtresse réalisée avec une précision d'horloger qui s'articule autour d'un patio principal, doté d'un portique sur ses trois côtés et d'un patio secondaire paysagé. Son langage architectural et décoratif correspond à un élégant baroque tardif, avec des éléments et influences néoclassiques. Les propriétaires actuels craignaient que cette dernière restauration du palais n'efface les empreintes du temps. Toutefois, grâce à un travail minutieux, l'esthétique originale de la construction a été préservée, tant sur la façade extérieure et les toits, qu'à l'intérieur. En outre, chaque pièce ajoutée a été bien pensée pour préserver au maximum l'essence historique de ce splendide palais italien.

Im Jahr 1770 errichtete der Architekt Cosimo Morelli diesen Palast in Piacenza. Es handelt sich um ein streng geplantes, meisterhaftes Bauwerk, das einen Innenhof mit drei Säulengängen und einen zweiten, begrünten Hof umgibt. Die architektonische und dekorative Ausdrucksweise ist von elegantem Spätbarock mit neoklassischen Einflüssen und Elementen geprägt. Die heutigen Besitzer fürchteten, dass der Palast durch die letzte Renovierung seine von der Entstehungszeit geprägte Ästhetik einbüßen könnte, aber durch eine sorgfältige Planung war es möglich, die originale Architektur des Gebäudes sowohl an Fassade und Dach als auch im Inneren zu erhalten. Alle neuen Objekte wurden mit großer Sorgfalt hinzugefügt, um die historische Essenz dieses wundervollen, italienischen Palastes zu bewahren.

Nel 1770 l'architetto Cosimo Morelli progettò questo palazzo nel centro storico di Piacenza. Si tratta di un capolavoro eseguito con rigorosa precisione e che si articola attorno ad un cortile centrale, porticato nei suoi tre lati, e un cortile secondario giardinato. Il suo linguaggio architettonico e decorativo risponde ad un elegante tardobarocco con elementi e influenze neoclassiche. Gli attuali proprietari temevano che in seguito a quest'ultima ristrutturazione il palazzo perdesse i suoi segni più caratteristici. Invece, grazie ad un minuzioso lavoro si è riusciti a conservare l'estetica originale della costruzione, sia della facciata esterna e dei tetti che degli interni. In questa nobile residenza, ed esattamente nel salone d'onore al piano rialzato, si è da poco insediata l'associazione Piacenza Arte con l'obiettivo di tenervi conferenze, concerti, salotti letterari ed iniziative culturali.

En 1770, el arquitecto Cosimo Morelli proyectó este palacio situado en Piacenza. Se trata de una obra maestra llevada a cabo con rigurosa precisión y que se articula en torno a un patio principal, porticado en sus tres lados, y un patio secundario ajardinado. Su lenguaje arquitectónico y decorativo responde a un elegante barroco tardío con elementos e influencias neoclásicas. Los propietarios actuales temían que con esta última restauración el palacio perdiese las huellas del tiempo, pero, gracias a un minucioso trabajo, se ha conseguido rescatar la estética original de la construcción, tanto de la fachada exterior y los tejados, como del interior. Además, cada pieza añadida se ha meditado cuidadosamente con objeto de preservar al máximo la esencia histórica de este espléndido palacio italiano.

MOHEN DESIGN INTERNATIONAL | SHANGHAI, CHINA

Website	www.mohen-design.com
Project	Commercial Office
Location	Shanghai, China
Year of completion	2006
Photo credits	Maoder Chou/Mohen Design International

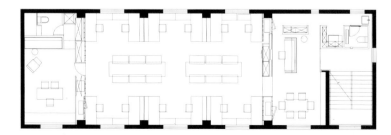

This office occupies three floors of a building located in the heart of Shanghai. The design encompasses classic decorative elements and modern architecture. The acrylic chandeliers and the elaborately embossed white panels convey a certain sense of originality as well as subtly accentuating the work ambience without causing distraction. In this way the functionality of certain elements, such as the large tables and the simple yet elegant drawing room, is not affected by the desire to create a different kind of space with certain classic features.

Diese Büroräume erstrecken sich über drei Stockwerke in einem Gebäude im Zentrum von Schanghai. Die Architekten vereinten in der Gestaltung klassische Elemente mit moderner Architektur. Die Kronleuchter aus Acryl und die weißen Platten mit aufwendig gearbeiteten Reliefs verleihen der Dekoration eine gewisse Originalität und unterstreichen zugleich die Arbeitsumgebung, ohne abzulenken. So ist die Funktionalität einiger Elemente – wie die langen Tische und der einfache, aber elegante Konferenzsaal – nicht unvereinbar mit dem Anspruch, eine ganz besondere Umgebung mit klassischen Anspielungen zu schaffen.

Esta oficina comprende los tres pisos de un edificio situado en el centro de Shanghai. A través de su diseño, los arquitectos han logrado aunar elementos clásicos de la decoración con la arquitectura moderna. Los *chandeliers* acrílicos que han diseñado o los paneles blancos con trabajosos relieves se han integrado en el ambiente para aportar un toque original a la vez que acentuar el ambiente de trabajo con la sutileza suficiente como para no ser causa de distracción. De este modo, la funcionalidad de algunos elementos, como las largas mesas o la sencilla pero elegante sala de reuniones, no está reñida con la voluntad de crear un espacio diferente, con reminiscencias clásicas puntuales.

Ce bureau englobe les trois étages d'un édifice situé au centre de Shanghai. Par le biais de leur design, les architectes sont parvenus à unir les éléments classiques de la décoration à l'architecture moderne. Les lustres conçus en acrylique ou les panneaux blancs aux reliefs travaillés s'intègrent à l'ambiance pour apporter une touche originale, tout en accentuant l'atmosphère de travail avec la subtilité nécessaire pour ne pas être cause de distraction. De cette manière, la fonctionnalité de certains éléments, à l'instar des grandes tables ou de la salle de réunion, simple mais élégante, n'est pas incompatible avec la volonté de créer un espace différent, ponctué de touches de réminiscences classiques.

Questo ufficio occupa i tre piani di un edificio situato nel centro di Shanghai. Mediante un'accurata progettazione, gli architetti hanno saputo riunire elementi decorativi classici ed inserirli in un contesto architettonico moderno. Gli *chandelier* in acrilico o i pannelli bianchi con elaborati rilievi sono stati integrati perfettamente nello spazio per dare un tocco di originalità, non stonando comunque all'interno di un ambiente di lavoro. In questo modo, la funzionalità di alcuni elementi come i lunghi tavoli o la semplice ma elegante sala riunioni non è in contraddizione con la volontà di creare uno spazio differente, dotato di alcune reminescenze classiche.

We have diversified
a practice that focuses on clients
wishing to pursue innovative
design strategies
we are committed to high
quality designs

MOHEN DESIGN INTERNATIONAL | SHANGHAI, CHINA

Website	www.mohen-design.com
Project	Parkside Bistro and Bar
Location	Shanghai, China
Year of completion	2007
Photo credits	Maoder Chou/Mohen Design International

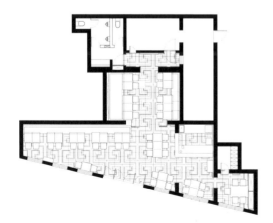

The colonial heritage of the city of Shanghai can still be seen in some of its streets. Hundreds of neo-baroque buildings still stand in a curious and cosmopolitan mix of styles, whose essence has been reflected in the design of the Parkside Bistro and Bar. Escaping from the traditional moldings, the ceiling has been decorated with brass tubes that draw an asymmetrical picture. The false finishes bring a historical touch to the gloss paint. The floor boasts a geometric design created from vinyl tiles that enrich the ensemble and recreate the luxurious character of the baroque style, although in a softer and more contemporary way.

Man kann das koloniale Erbe Schanghais noch in einigen Straßen erkennen. In einer interessanten, kosmopolitischen Stilmischung wurden in der Stadt noch hunderte von neobarocken Gebäuden erhalten, deren stilistische Essenz sich auch in der Gestaltung des Parkside Bistro and Bar widerspiegelt. Der traditionelle Deckenstuck wurde durch Messingrohre ersetzt, die ein asymmetrisches Muster bilden. Falsche Verkleidungen lassen die glänzende Wandfarbe historisch wirken. Der Boden ist von einem geometrischen Vinylmosaik bedeckt, das den Raum bereichert und einen luxuriösen Barockstil schafft, der jedoch sanft und zeitgemäß wirkt.

La herencia colonial de la ciudad de Shanghai aún se muestra en algunas de sus calles. Cientos de edificios neobarrocos todavía se erigen en una curiosa y cosmopolita mezcla de estilos, cuya esencia se ha querido reflejar en el diseño del Parkside Bistro and Bar. Escapando de las tradicionales molduras, el techo ha sido decorado con tubos de latón que crean un dibujo asimétrico. Los acabados falsos aportan un toque histórico a la pintura brillante. Para el suelo se ha utilizado un diseño geométrico con teselas de vinilo que enriquecen el conjunto y recrean el carácter lujoso del estilo barroco, aunque de una manera más suave y contemporánea.

L'héritage colonial de la ville de Shanghai est encore visible dans certaines de ses rues. Une centaine d'édifices néo baroques s'élèvent encore dans un mélange de styles cosmopolites et insolites dont l'essence se reflète volontairement dans le design du Parkside Bistro and Bar. Fuyant les traditionnels moulures, le plafond est décoré avec des tubes de laiton qui créent un dessin asymétrique. Les fausses finitions apportent une touche historique à la peinture brillante. Pour le sol, on a utilisé un design géométrique avec des carreaux en vinyle qui enrichissent l'ensemble et recréent le caractère luxueux du style baroque, toutefois plus en douceur et avec une contemporanéité accrue.

Il passato coloniale della città di Shanghai è ancora evidente in alcune sue strade. Centinaia di edifici neobarocchi si ergono ancora in una curiosa e cosmopolita mescolanza di stili, che è stata colta e ben rappresentata nell'arredamento del Parkside Bistro and Bar. Allontanandosi dalle tradizionali modanature, il soffitto è stato decorato con tubi di ottone che creano un disegno asimmetrico. Le finiture false apportano un tocco storico alla pittura brillante. Per il pavimento è stato usato un disegno geometrico con tessere di vinile che arricchiscono l'insieme e ricreano il carattere lussuoso dello stile barocco, anche se in maniera più leggera e contemporanea.

PATRICK JOUIN | PARIS, FRANCE

Website	www.patrickjouin.com
Project	Gilt
Location	New York, United States
Year of completion	2005
Photo credits	Eric Laignel

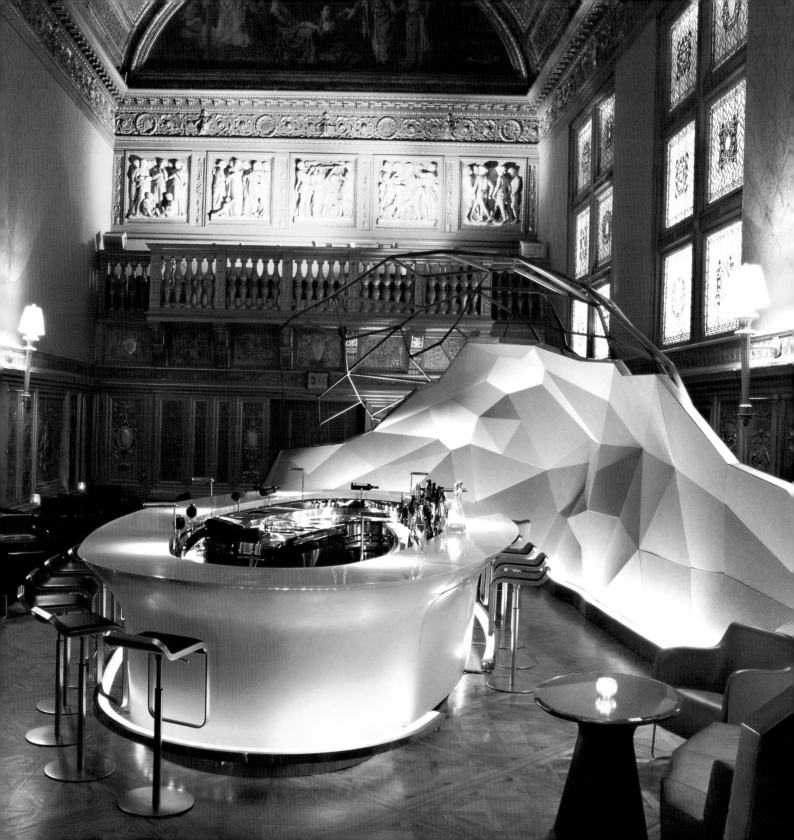

The designer Patrick Jouin's work in the Gold Room Bar disproves the general belief that blending modern and classical styles creates conflict. This is one of the spaces of the Gilt project which comprises a bar, restaurant and wine cellar and is located in the patio of New York's Palace Hotel, set in the historic Villard House. The futuristic curved bar illuminated from below and a spectacular geode shaped structure in sharp contrast to the classic windows are housed within the walls of the Gold Room Bar which boast elaborate molding and murals inspired by a concept somewhere between the Renaissance and the Baroque.

Das Aufeinandertreffen von Klassisch und Modern muss nicht disharmonisch wirken, wie der Designer Patrick Jouin in der Gold Room Bar beweist. Es handelt sich um einen der Räume des Gilts, ein Großprojekt, das eine Bar, ein Restaurant und einen Weinkeller in dem Hof des Hotels Palace in New York in dem historischen Villard House einschließt. Die Wände der Golden Bar, bedeckt mit edlem Gesims und Wandgemälden, die von einem Stil zwischen Renaissance und Barock inspiriert sind, umgeben das wichtigste Element des Saals: eine futuristische, kurvenförmige, von unten beleuchtete Stange und eine geodenförmige Struktur, die mitten in der Bar eine auffallende Alternative zu den klassischen Glasfenstern bildet.

El encuentro entre lo clásico y lo moderno no siempre resulta conflictivo y así lo ha demostrado el diseñador Patrick Jouin en el Gold Room Bar. Éste es uno de los espacios que integran Gilt, un amplio proyecto que aúna bar, restaurante y bodega, y está situado en el patio del Hotel Palace de Nueva York, ubicado en la histórica Villard House. Las paredes del Gold Room Bar, que muestran molduras elaboradas y murales inspirados en un estilo a medio camino entre el Renacimiento y el Barroco, rodean a los protagonistas de la sala: una barra curva futurista, iluminada desde abajo, y una estructura con forma de geoda que contrasta con las clásicas vidrieras y se muestra espectacular en el centro del bar.

L'alliance du classique et du moderne n'est pas toujours conflictuelle comme le démontre le designer Patrick Jouin dans le Gold Room Bar. C'est un des espaces qui intègre le Gilt, un grand projet englobant bar, restaurant et cave, et qui est situé dans le patio de l'Hôtel Palace de New York, installé dans l'historique Villard House. Les murs du Gold Room Bar, parés de moulures élaborées et de peintures murales inspirées d'un style à mi-chemin entre la renaissance et le Baroque, entourent les protagonistes de la salle : un bar futuriste tout en courbes, éclairé par le bas, et une structure en forme de géode qui contraste avec les verrières classiques et prend des allures spectaculaires au centre du bar.

L'incontro tra il classico e il moderno non è sempre stridente e così lo ha ben dimostrato il designer Patrick Jouin nel Gold Room Bar. Questo è uno degli spazi che inglobano Gilt, un ampio progetto che mette insieme bar, ristorante e cantina; il tutto situato nel cortile dell'Hotel Palace di New York, all'interno dello storico edificio di Villard House. Le pareti del Gold Room Bar, che mostrano modanature elaborate e murales ispirati ad uno stile a metà strada tra il Rinascimento e il Barocco, circondano i protagonisti della sala: un bancone curvo e futurista, illuminato dal basso, e una spettacolare struttura a forma di geode, in contrasto con le classiche vetrate, posta al centro del bar.

PERIPHERIQUES ARCHITECTES | PARIS, FRANCE

Website	www.peripheriques-architectes.com
Project	Nouveau Casino
Location	Paris, France
Year of completion	2002
Photo credits	Luc Boegly

The structure that surrounds this club has an industrial aesthetic, while the design of the space concealed inside is based on baroque eclecticism. The Nouveau Casino has been especially designed to have a low capacity, in particularly for holding concerts. While the central space is dimly lit, the light is reflected in the walls and part of the ceiling, which is clad in rigid triangular metal sheets. This material reflects the videocreations that accompany the music and which create a changing and original aesthetic. The final touches come from the curved form of the bar and the majestic chandeliers that decorate the ceiling.

Dieser Club ist von einer Struktur von industrieller Ästhetik umgeben, die in ihrem Inneren einen von barockem Eklektizismus geprägten Raum beherbergt. Das Nouveau Casino wurde vor allem als ein Lokal für kleinere Veranstaltungen, speziell Konzerte, gestaltet. Der zentrale Bereich ist nur spärlich beleuchtet, und das Licht spiegelt sich an den Wänden und an Teilen der Decke wider, die mit starren, dreieckigen Blechplatten verkleidet sind. Dieses Material reflektiert auch die Videokreationen, die die Musik begleiten – eine originelle Idee, die für stete Veränderung sorgt. Den Schlusspunkt bilden die gebogene Bar und die majestätischen Kronleuchter an der Decke.

La estructura que envuelve este club tiene una estética industrial, en su interior se esconde un espacio cuyo diseño se basa en un eclecticismo barroco. El Nouveau Casino ha sido concebido, sobre todo, como un local de aforo reducido, destinado especialmente a conciertos. El espacio central queda escasamente iluminado, mientras que la luz se refleja en las paredes y parte del techo, recubiertos de rígidas chapas triangulares. Este material refleja las videocreaciones que acompañan la música y que crean una estética cambiante y original. El toque final lo ponen las formas curvas de la barra y los majestuosos chandeliers que decoran el techo del local.

La structure qui enveloppe ce club revêt une esthétique industrielle qui cache à l'intérieur un espace dont le design est basé sur un éclecticisme baroque. Le Nouveau Casino a été surtout conçu comme un établissement de capacité d'accueil réduite, destiné avant tout aux concerts. L'espace central est faiblement éclairé, tandis que la lumière se reflète sur les murs et une partie du plafond, recouverts de plaques rigides triangulaires. Cette matière reflète les créations vidéo qui accompagnent la musique, créant une esthétique fluctuante et originale. La touche finale est apportée par les formes courbes du bar et les majestueux lustres qui décorent le plafond de l'établissement.

La struttura che avvolge questo club presenta un'estetica industriale e al suo interno si nasconde uno spazio il cui design si basa su un eclettismo barocco. Il Nouveau Casino è stato concepito, soprattutto, come un locale a capienza ridotta, destinato specialmente a piccoli concerti. Lo spazio centrale rimane scarsamente illuminato, mentre la luce si riflette nelle pareti e parte del soffitto, ricoperte di rigide lastre di acciaio triangolari. Questo materiale riflette inoltre le videocreazioni che accompagnano la musica e che creano un'ambientazione cangiante ed originale. Il tocco finale è dato dalle forme curve del banco e dai maestosi chandelier che decorano il soffitto del locale.

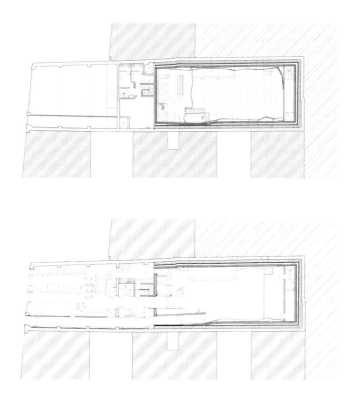

PHILIPPE STARCK | PARIS, FRANCE

Website	www.philippe-starck.com
Project	Faena Hotel
Location	Buenos Aires, Argentina
Year of completion	2004
Photo credits	Nikolas Koenig

Philippe Starck once again delves into his repertoire of excess and luxury for the design of the Faena Hotel, located in El Porteño, a brick building over a hundred years old which features a 260 ft corridor complete with an endless red carpet and gold velvet curtained walls. Impressive chandeliers and candle holders crown the ceilngs and decorate the tables of the bar and restaurant, which blend with the capitone upholstered armchairs and sofas with gold details and exquisite pieces of glassware. The bathroom is one of the most spectacular rooms where tuscan marble covers the walls and the swan shaped tapes are reflected in the large mirror with an engraved silver frame.

Philippe Starck entfaltet sein ganzes Repertoire an Übertreibung und Luxus bei der Gestaltung des Faena Hotels in El Porteño, einem über hundert Jahre alten Ziegelsteingebäude. Nach dem spektakulären Eingangsbereich betritt man einen 80 Meter langen Flur mit einem unendlich scheinenden, roten Teppich, dessen Wände mit majestätischen Gardinen aus goldenem Samt behangen sind. Mächtige Kronleuchter und Kerzenhalter hängen von den Decken und dekorieren die Tische der Bar und des Restaurants. Hinzu kommen Sessel und Sofas mit rautenförmig gesteppten, goldenen Polstern und wertvolle Glasobjekte. Einer der prachtvollsten Räume ist das Bad, in dem sich die mit Marmor aus der Toscana verkleideten Wände und schwanenförmige Armaturen in einem großen, gravierten Spiegel mit silbernem Rahmen wiederfinden.

Philippe Starck despliega otra vez todo su repertorio de excesos y lujos para el diseño del Faena Hotel, ubicado en El Porteño, un edificio de ladrillo con más de cien años de antigüedad. A la espectacular entrada sigue un pasillo de 80 metros con una interminable alfombra de color rojo y cuyas paredes se han revestido con majestuosas cortinas de terciopelo dorado. Impresionantes *chandeliers* y portavelas coronan los techos y decoran las mesas del bar y del restaurante, unidos a las butacas y los sofás tapizados en capitoné con detalles dorados y a exquisitas piezas de cristalería. Una de las estancias más espectaculares es el baño, donde el mármol toscano reviste las paredes y los grifos en forma de cisne se reflejan en un gran espejo con un marco grabado y de color plata.

Philippe Starck déploie une fois de plus son répertoire d'excès et de luxes dans le design du Faena Hotel, situé à El Porteño, un édifice en briques plus que centenaire. L'entrée spectaculaire est suivie d'un couloir de 80 mètres doté d'un interminable tapis rouge et de murs habillés de majestueux rideaux en velours doré. D'impressionnants lustres et bougeoirs couronnent les plafonds et décorent les tables du bar et du restaurant, conjugués aux fauteuils et divans capitonnés ornés de détails dorés et à de ravissantes pièces de verrerie. La salle de bains est une des pièces les plus spectaculaires où le marbre toscan revêt les murs et où les robinets en forme de cygne se reflètent dans un grand miroir doté d'un cadre gravé blanc et argent.

Il designer francese Philippe Stark sfoggia ancora una volta il suo repertorio di soluzioni ardite e eccessi decorativi per il design del Faena Hotel, ubicato ne El Porteño, un edificio in mattoni costruito agli inizi del 1900 a Buenos Aires. All'imponente ingresso fa seguito un corridoio di 80 metri con un interminabile tappeto di colore rosso e le cui pareti sono state rivestite con tende drappeggiate di velluto dorato. Mirabili *chandelier* e portacandele coronano i soffitti e adornano i tavoli del bar e del ristorante. Oltre alle poltrone e ai divani in capitonnè, con dettagli dorati, si fanno notare alcuni pregevoli pezzi di cristalleria. Uno degli ambienti che più attira l'attenzione è il bagno, con pareti rivestite di marmo toscano verde e porpora; i rubinetti a forma di cigno si riflettono in un grande specchio con cornice incisa e di color argento.

PHILIPPE STARCK | PARIS, FRANCE

Website	www.philippe-starck.com
Project	Hudson Hotel
Location	New York, United States
Year of completion	2005
Photo credits	Mihail Moldovenau

An unbridled mix of styles leads to another universe created by Philipe Starck which impregnates the Hudson Hotel in New York, especially the bar zone. An extravagant Versace armchair with golden swans sculptured into armrests creates a curious contrast with the adjacent log bench. The glass floor is illuminated from below and the ceiling is decorated with a superb work or art by Francisco Clemente. This space leads on to a very peculiar universe where a modern and futuristic aesthetic converges with Louis XV inspired furniture resulting in an ideal place in which to relax by candle light.

Eine ungestüme Stilmischung führt uns in ein Universum, das von Philippe Starck geschaffen wurde und das Hotel Hudson in New York erfüllt, insbesondere im Bereich der Bar. Schon beim Eintreten sieht man einen extravaganten Sessel von Versace mit goldenen Schwänen als Armlehnen, der einen interessanten Gegensatz zu der daneben stehenden Bank aus einem Baumstamm bildet. Der Glasboden wird von unten beleuchtet und die Decke mit einem wundervollen Gemälde des Künstlers Francesco Clemente geschmückt. Dieser Raum ist das Entrée zu einer Designwelt, in der eine moderne, vom Weltraum inspirierte Ästhetik mit Möbeln kombiniert wird, die vom Louis XV-Stil inspiriert sind. So entsteht eine ideale Umgebung, wie geschaffen, um sich bei Kerzenlicht zu entspannen.

Una desenfrenada mezcla de estilos nos conduce a un universo que parte de nuevo de la mente de Philippe Starck e impregna el hotel Hudson de Nueva York, especialmente la zona del bar. Nada más entrar, una extravagante butaca Versace con cisnes dorados esculpidos a modo de reposabrazos forma un curioso contraste con un banco hecho con un tronco de madera dispuesto a su lado. El suelo de cristal está iluminado desde abajo y en el techo destaca una fantástica pintura obra del artista Francesco Clemente. Este espacio conduce a un universo muy peculiar donde una estética moderna e incluso espacial confluye con muebles inspirados en el estilo Luis XV para lograr una atmósfera idónea en la que disfrutar y relajarse a la luz de las velas.

Un mélange de styles effréné nous entraîne dans un nouvel univers, fruit de l'imagination de Philippe Starck, et qui imprègne l'hôtel Hudson de New York, notamment dans la zone du bar. Dès l'entrée, un fauteuil extravagant de Versace doté d'accoudoirs en forme de cygnes dorés sculptés forme un étonnant contraste avec, juste à côté, un banc réalisé dans un tronc de bois. Le sol en verre est éclairé par le bas et le plafond met en relief une peinture fantastique, œuvre de l'artiste Francesco Clemente. Cet espace conduit vers un univers très particulier où une esthétique moderne et même spatiale côtoie des meubles inspirés du style Louis XV pour créer une atmosphère idéale où passer un bon moment et se relaxer à la lueur des bougies.

Uno sfrenato mix di stili ci conduce ad un universo scaturito nuovamente dalla mente di Philippe Starck che impregna l'hotel Hudson di New York, specialmente la zona del bar. Non appena si entra, una stravagante poltrona Versace con cigni dorati scolpiti a mo' di poggiabraccia forma un curioso contrasto con un bancone ricavato da un tronco di legno collocato proprio accanto. Il pavimento di cristallo viene illuminato dal basso e nel soffitto spicca un fantastico dipinto, opera dell'artista Francesco Clemente. Questo spazio dà accesso ad un ambiente molto peculiare, con un'estetica moderna e persino spaziale che dialoga con mobili ispirati allo stile Luigi XV. Il tutto per ottenere la migliore delle atmosfere, dove rilassarsi a lume di candela.

PHILIPPE STARCK | PARIS, FRANCE

Website	www.philippe-starck.com
Project	Kong Restaurant
Location	Paris, France
Year of completion	2003
Photo credits	Patricia Bailer

Kong bar-restaurant occupies the top two floors of the Kenzo building and boasts spectacular views of the Pont Neuf. In this privileged space, Phillipe Starck has once again used his imagination and created an ambience which combines historic France and modern day Japan. Printed asian faces adorn the Louis XV inspired transparent seats and armchairs as well as the glass walls which separate the tables from the bar. Transparency is one of the key themes of the decoration and brings the furniture into harmony with the immense glass dome roof which crowns the building.

Le bar-restaurant Kong occupe les deux derniers étages de l'édifice Kenzo d'où l'on jouit de vues spectaculaires sur le Pont Neuf. Dans cet espace privilégié, Philippe Starck a, une fois de plus, déployé son imagination pour recréer une atmosphère à mi-chemin entre la France historique et le Japon actuel. De multiples visages, asiatiques pour la plupart, vous observent depuis les sièges et fauteuils transparents inspirés du style Louis XV, ainsi que depuis les vitres qui séparent les tables du bar, surfaces où ils ont été imprimés. La notion de transparence se répète dans toute la décoration de l'espace, harmonisant ainsi le mobilier à la grande coupole de verre qui couronne l'édifice et sert de toiture au restaurant.

Das Restaurant und die Bar Kong befinden sich auf den oberen Etagen des Gebäudes Kenzo, von wo man einen wundervollen Blick auf die Pont Neuf hat. In diesem schönen Lokal hat Philippe Starck wieder einmal seiner Phantasie freien Lauf gelassen und eine Umgebung geschaffen, die eine Verbindung zwischen der französischen Geschichte und dem heutigen Japan herstellt. Zahlreiche meist asiatische Gesichter beobachten von transparenten Stühlen und Sesseln im Stil Louis XV aus die Gäste. Auch die Glaswände, die den Barbereich abtrennen, zeigen diese Gesichter. Die Idee der Transparenz wiederholt sich in der gesamten Dekoration des Lokals und verbindet die Möbel harmonisch mit der großen Glaskuppel, die das Gebäude krönt und gleichzeitig die Decke des Restaurants bildet.

Il bar-ristorante Kong occupa gli ultimi due piani del Kenzo building, da cui si gode una magnifica vista panoramica del Pont Neuf. In questo spazio privilegiato, Philippe Starck ha dato ancora una volta libero sfogo alla sua immaginazione per ricreare un ambiente a metà strada tra la Francia degli anni 50 e il Giappone attuale. Nelle sedie e poltrone trasparenti ispirate allo stile Luigi XV, così come nei vetri che separano i tavoli del bar, sono stati incisi dei volti, per la maggior parte asiatici, che sembrano osservare i commensali. L'idea di trasparenza è costante in tutto l'arredamento ed è presente anche nella grande cupola vetrata che corona l'edificio e che serve pure da copertura al ristorante.

El bar-restaurante Kong ocupa las dos últimas plantas del edificio Kenzo desde donde brinda unas vistas espectaculares sobre el Pont Neuf. En este espacio privilegiado, Philippe Starck ha desplegado una vez más su imaginación para recrear un ambiente a medio camino entre la Francia histórica y el Japón actual. Múltiples rostros, la mayoría asiáticos, observan desde las sillas y butacas transparentes inspiradas en el estilo Luis XV, así como desde los cristales que separan las mesas del bar, superficies en las que han sido impresas. La idea de transparencia se repite en toda la decoración del espacio y armoniza el mobiliario con la gran cúpula acristalada que corona el edificio y que también sirve de cubierta al restaurante.

PHILIPPE STARCK | PARIS, FRANCE

Website	www.philippe-starck.com
Project	Maison Baccarat
Location	Paris, France
Year of completion	2004
Photo credits	Claude Weber

The French designer Phillipe Starck has been the author of the new decoration of this buiding dating back to 1895 and which now has been converted into the new headquarters of the renowned glass firm Baccarat. The obviously baroque aesthetic has filled this palace, in whose interior hang majestic chandeliers which illuminate the glass pieces of the boutique and of the museum, where glass protects the oldest and most precious pieces of the house. The restaurant, managed by the Chef Thierry Burlot, follows the same line as the other rooms and combines white and gold in the main dining hall, and black and pink under a capitone upholstered ceiling in the private lounge.

Der französische Designer Philippe Starck ist der Schöpfer der neuen Dekoration dieses Gebäudes aus dem Jahr 1895, das heute der Sitz der bekannten Kristallerie Baccarat ist. Die deutlich barocke Ästhetik überflutet den Palast, in dessen Innenräumen majestätische Kronleuchter hängen, die das Kristall im Shop und im Museum illuminieren, in deren Vitrinen die ältesten und wertvollsten Stücke des Hauses ausgestellt werden. Das Restaurant, das von Küchenchef Thierry Burlot geleitet wird, folgt der gleichen Ästhetik wie die anderen Säle; es dominieren Weiß und Gold in einem eleganten Hauptsaal, Schwarz und Rosa unter einer mit einem gesteppten Rautenmuster gepolsterten Decke in einem privaten Saal.

El diseñador francés Philippe Starck ha sido el artífice de la nueva decoración de este edificio construido en 1895 y que ahora se ha convertido en la sede de la conocida firma de cristalería Baccarat. La clara estétca barroca ha inundado este palacete, en cuyo interior cuelgan majestuosos *chandeliers* que iluminan las piezas de cristal tanto de la tienda como del museo, donde las vitrinas resguardan las piezas más antiguas y preciadas de la casa. El restaurante, que regenta el chef Thierry Burlot, sigue la misma estética que las demás salas y combina el blanco y el dorado en la elegante sala principal, y el negro y el rosa bajo un techo tapizado en capitoné en la sala privada.

Le designer français Philippe Starck est l'artisan de la nouvelle décoration de cet édifice construit en 1895, devenu aujourd'hui le siège de la célèbre cristallerie Baccarat. L'esthétique clairement baroque inonde ce petit palais, à l'intérieur duquel pendent de majestueux lustres qui illuminent les œuvres en cristal de la boutique et du musée où les vitrines protègent les pièces les plus anciennes et les plus prestigieuses de la maison. Le restaurant, dirigé par le chef Thierry Burlot, suit la même ligne esthétique que les autres salles, en conjuguant le blanc et le doré dans l'élégante salle principale, et dans la salle privée, le noir et rose, sous un plafond capitonné.

L'affermato designer francese Philippe Starck è stato l'artefice della nuova veste di questo edificio costruito nel 1895 e trasformato adesso nella sede del noto marchio di cristalleria Baccarat. Una chiara estetica barocca ha inondato questo palazzo, nei cui interni pendono maestosi *chandelier* che illuminano gli oggetti di cristallo sia del negozio che del museo, dove le vetrine custodiscono i pezzi più antichi e di valore della maison. Il ristorante, gestito dallo chef Thierry Burlot, segue la stessa estetica delle altre stanze e combina il bianco e l'oro nell'elegante sala principale, e il nero e il rosa sotto un soffitto tappezzato in capitonnè nella sala privata.

PLAYGROUND MELBOURNE | MELBOURNE, AUSTRALIA

Website	www.playgroundmelbourne.com
Project	Baroq House
Location	Melbourne, Australia
Year of completion	2004
Photo credits	Shania Shegedyn

This bar-lounge oozes intimacy and sophistication. It is somwhere to converse and interact in a comfortable and visually attractive ambience. The baroque theme is evident throughout the whole place in the decorative detail, materials and colors used. Inspite of this clear style, the existing structure of the space was preserved and simplified as much as possible. The particular style of Baroq House has been classified by its creators as minimalist baroque and is defined by a blend of sophisticated and luxurious decoration, in a space which successfully reproduces the interior of a mansion with its lounges and hallways.

Edel und intim. So könnte man diese „Bar-Lounge" definieren, die mit ihrer freundlichen und visuell anziehenden Atmosphäre zur Unterhaltung einlädt. Die barocke Thematik, auf der das Design basiert, zeigt sich im gesamten Lokal an den Dekorationsstücken, an einigen Materialien und an der Farbe. Trotz der klaren stilistischen Absicht respektierte man bei der Gestaltung die existierende Struktur so weit wie möglich und versuchte, sie stark zu vereinfachen. So erreichte man diesen besonderen Stil des Baroq Haus, der von seinen Schöpfern auf den Namen minimalistischer Barock getauft wurde. Eine Mischung aus edler, luxuriöser Dekoration in einer Umgebung, die die Salons und Empfangshallen einer Villa nachempfindet.

Íntimo y sofisticado. Así se podría definir este *bar-lounge* que propone un espacio donde dialogar e interactuar en un ambiente acogedor y visualmente atractivo. La temática barroca, en la que se ha basado su diseño, se expresa en todo el local por medio de los detalles decorativos, algunos materiales y los colores. A pesar de esta clara intención estilística, en su diseño se respetó al máximo la estructura existente del espacio y se intentó simplificarla al máximo. Así se logró el estilo particular del Baroq House, bautizado por sus creadores como un minimalismo barroco. Una mezcla de decoración sofisticada y lujosa en un espacio que reproduce con sus salones y vestíbulos el interior de una mansión.

Intime et sophistiqué. C'est ainsi que l'on peut définir ce *bar-lounge* qui propose un espace où dialoguer et converser dans une atmosphère visuellement accueillante et intéressante. La thématique baroque, base de ce design, est présente dans tout l'établissement grâce à des détails décoratifs et à certains matériaux et couleurs. En dehors de cette expression stylistique évidente, le design respecte au maximum la structure spatiale existante, en essayant de la simplifier le plus possible. Ceci aboutit au style particulier de la « Baroq House », baptisée par ses créateurs de minimalisme baroque. Un mélange de décoration sophistiquée et luxueuse dans un espace qui reproduit, avec ses salons et vestibules, l'intérieur d'une demeure.

Intimo e raffinato. Così si potrebbe definire questo *bar-lounge* che propone uno spazio dove dialogare e interagire, all'interno di un ambiente accogliente e visivamente attraente. I motivi barocchi, che ne hanno ispirato l'arredamento, si esprimono in tutto il locale mediante i dettagli decorativi, alcuni materiali adoperati e i colori. Nonostante questa evidente intenzione stilistica, nel progettare questo locale si è rispettata al massimo la preesistente distribuzione dello spazio cercando nel limite del possibile di semplificarla. Così è nato lo stile particolare del Baroq House, battezzato dai suoi creatori come un minimalismo barocco. Un arredamento che mescola lusso e raffinatezza in uno spazio dove i suoi saloni e gli atri riproducono l'interno di una mansione.

RICARDAS VYSNIAUSKAS | VILNIUS, LITHUANIA

Website	www.ricardasvysniauskas.lt
Project	Universal
Location	Kaliningrad, Russia
Year of completion	2004
Photo credits	Modestas Ezerskis, Narimantas Serksnys

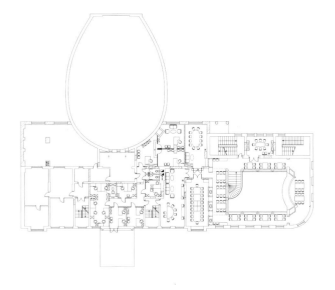

After several attempts at designing a club whose aesthetics would recreate a luxurious and bohemian atmosphere without being too exclusive, architect Ricardas Vysniauskas has achieved a curious, fun and spectacular space. Its charm lies in the mix of creative moments, in other words, the co-existence — in a single space — of elements that have been salvaged from their first transformation together with others that have been added or replaced. All this achieves an undoubtedly neoclassical environment that impregnates this nightclub. The angels hanging from the sky blue ceiling invite people to enter this place, whose baroque air also recreates an old cabaret.

Nach mehreren Versuchen, einen Club mit einer luxuriösen, unkonventionellen Atmosphäre zu schaffen, ohne dass dieser zu exklusiv wirkt, schuf Ricardas Vysniauskas dieses interessante, unterhaltsame und auffallende Lokal. Sein Zauber liegt in der Mischung kreativer Momente, also dem Zusammenleben von Elementen aus unterschiedlichen Gestaltungsperioden, von denen immer wieder einige hinzugefügt bzw. ersetzt wurden. So entstand ein neoklassischer Stil, der diesen Nightclub prägt. Die Engel, die unter der himmelblauen Decke hängen, laden zum Eintritt in das Lokal ein, dessen barocke Umgebung auch an ein altes Kabarett erinnert.

Tras varios intentos por lograr un club cuya estética recreara un ambiente lujoso y bohemio sin resultar demasiado exclusivo, el arquitecto Ricardas Vysniauskas ha logrado un espacio curioso, divertido y espectacular. Su encanto reside en la mezcla de momentos creativos, es decir, la convivencia —en un mismo espacio— de elementos que han sido rescatados de su primera transformación junto con otros que han ido añadiéndose o sustituyéndose. Todo este conjunto logra, sin duda, un ambiente neoclásico que impregna este *night club*. Los ángeles que cuelgan del techo bajo el celestial color azul invitan a entrar en este local, cuyo aire barroco recrea también un antiguo cabaret.

Après avoir essayé plusieurs fois de créer un club dont l'esthétique recréerait une atmosphère de luxe et bohème sans être trop exclusive, l'architecte Ricardas Vysniauskas a réalisé un espace étonnant, amusant et spectaculaire. Son charme réside dans le mélange d'instants créatifs, notamment, la convivialité —au sein d'un même espace— et d'éléments récupérés de sa première transformation à côté d'autres qui s'y sont ajoutés ou substitués. Tout cet ensemble crée, indubitablement, une ambiance néoclassique qui imprègne ce *night club*. Les anges suspendus au plafond sous la voûte céleste bleu azur invitent à entrer dans cet établissement dont les allures baroques recréent également l'atmosphère d'un ancien cabaret.

Dopo vari tentativi di realizzare un club il cui look ricreasse un ambiente lussuoso e bohémien senza però risultare troppo esclusivo, l'architetto Ricardas Vysniauskas ha dato vita a uno spazio curioso, divertente e spettacolare. Il suo fascino risiede nella mescolanza di momenti creativi, cioè, la coesistenza —in uno stesso spazio— di elementi recuperati dalla prima trasformazione assieme ad altri che sono stati aggiunti o sostituiti. Nel complesso tutti questi elementi danno vita ad un ambiente neoclassico che pervade l'intero *night club*. Gli angeli appesi al soffitto sotto un celestiale colore blu invitano ad entrare in questo locale, la cui aria barocca sembra quella di un vecchio cabaret.

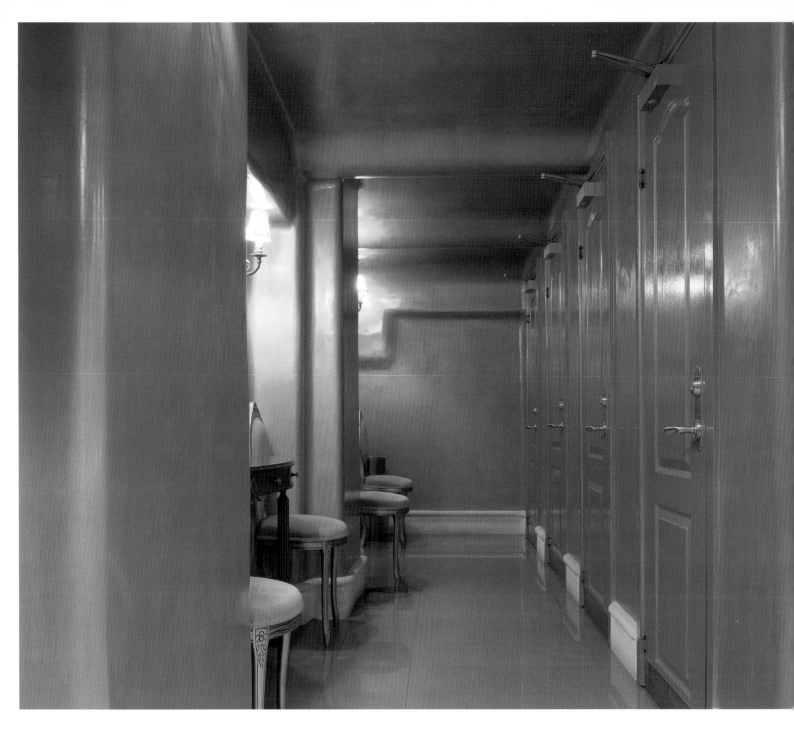

SLDESIGN | PHILADELPHIA, UNITED STATES

Website	www.sldesign.com
Project	Amalia
Location	New York, United States
Year of completion	2007
Photo credits	Peter Paige

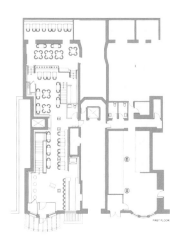

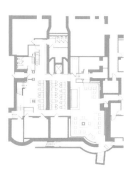

This restaurant owes its decadent and romantic appearance to the original materials of the space and the new decorative elements. The existing brick or stone walls contrast with the wooden panels, the hand-painted wallpaper and the Murano glass chandeliers. These, together with the oak wood floor and the flickering light from the candles, evoke the opulence and distinction of a grand European palace. The new decorative elements were conceived as insertions into the old structures, making it possible to differentiate the two and perceive them separately within the same space.

Das dekadente, romantische Aussehen dieses Restaurants ist auf die originelle Materialmischung im Lokal und auf neue Dekorationselemente zurückzuführen. Die Wände des Originalgebäudes sind aus Ziegel- oder Naturstein und bilden einen Kontrast zu den Holzpaneelen, den handgemalten Tapeten und den Kronleuchtern aus Muranoglas. In Kombination mit dem Fußboden aus Eiche und dem flackernden Kerzenlicht beschwören sie die Pracht und Noblesse der großen, europäischen Paläste herauf. Die neuen Dekorationselemente wirken wie Einfügungen innerhalb der alten Strukturen, so dass man sie gut im gleichen Raum erkennen und unterscheiden kann.

El aspecto decadente y romántico de este restaurante se debe a la mezcla de los materiales originales del local y los nuevos elementos decorativos. Las paredes de ladrillo o de piedra ya existentes contrastan con los paneles de madera, los papeles de pared pintados a mano y los *chandeliers* de cristal de Murano. Éstos, junto con el suelo de madera de roble y la luz parpadeante de las velas, evocan la opulencia y la distinción propias de los grandes palacios europeos. Los nuevos elementos decorativos son concebidos como inserciones dentro de las viejas estructuras, lo cual permite diferenciarlos y percibirlos por separado en un mismo espacio.

L'aspect décadent et romantique de ce restaurant réside dans la combinaison des matériaux d'origine de l'établissement et des nouveaux éléments décoratifs. Les murs en brique ou en pierre, existants auparavant, contrastent avec les panneaux de bois, les papiers muraux peints à la main et les lustres de cristal de Murano. Ces derniers, associés au sol de bois de chêne et à la lumière scintillante des bougies, évoquent l'opulence et l'élégance propre aux palais européens. Les nouveaux éléments décoratifs, sciemment insérés au cœur des anciennes structures, sont ainsi différenciés et perçus individuellement dans un espace commun.

L'aspetto decadente e romantico di questo ristorante è frutto dell'abbinamento dei materiali originali del locale e dei nuovi elementi decorativi. Le pareti in mattoni o pietra già esistenti contrastano con i pannelli di legno, le carte da parati dipinte a mano e i *chandelier* in vetro di Murano. Quest'ultimi, assieme al pavimento in legno di rovere e alla luce sfavillante delle candele, evocano l'opulenza e la distinzione proprie dei grandi palazzi europei. I nuovi elementi decorativi sono stati concepiti come inserimenti nelle vecchie strutture; questo accorgimento consente di differenziarli e percepirli separatamente nello stesso spazio.

STUDIO 63 ARCHITECTURE & DESIGN | FLORENCE, ITALY

Website	www.studio63.it
Project	Sixty Hotel
Location	Riccione, Italy
Year of completion	2006
Photo credits	Yael Pincus

The Sixty Hotel represents the first venture into the hotel market for the owner of the fashion brand Miss Sixty. The architecture and design reflect a search for innovation, as well as the latest trends. The reinvented classical touches can be appreciated in the hall, whose walls are clad in a mosaic with elegantly gold baroque motifs. The refined lines of the reception desk and the bar combine with this finish and with details such as the modern chandelier or the photograph that occupies the entire lateral wall above the sofas in the lobby. A modern sophistication characterizes the entrance to the hotel; a reflection of the bold spirit of youth fashion.

Das Sixty Hotel ist das erste Hotel, das von der Modemarke Miss Sixty geschaffen wurde. Die Architektur und Raumgestaltung sind von innovativer Kreativität und aktuellen Trends geprägt. Die Halle wurde in einem neu erfundenen, klassischen Stil dekoriert, ihre Wände mit einem eleganten, goldenen Mosaik mit barocken Motiven verkleidet. Die klaren Linien der Rezeption und der Bar verbinden sich mit diesen Verkleidungen und einzelnen Elementen wie dem modernen Kronleuchter und der Fotografie, die die gesamte Seitenwand über den Sofas der Lobby einnimmt. Diese moderne Noblesse prägt den Eingangsbereich des Hotels und vermittelt so die gewagte Linie der jugendlichen Mode des Hauses.

El Sixty Hotel es la primera aventura en el sector hotelero que ha llevado a cabo el propietario de la marca de moda Miss Sixty. Su arquitectura y diseño reflejan la búsqueda de la innovación y la apuesta por las últimas tendencias. Las pinceladas de un estilo clásico reinventado se evidencian en el hall, cuyas paredes están recubiertas de un mosaico con motivos barrocos en un elegante dorado. Las líneas depuradas del mostrador y la barra se mezclan con este revestimiento y con detalles como el moderno chandelier o la fotografía que ocupa toda la pared lateral, sobre los sofás del lobby. Una moderna sofisticación caracteriza la entrada de este hotel, reflejo del espíritu atrevido de la moda juvenil.

Le Sixty Hotel est la première aventure dans le secteur hôtelier réalisée par le propriétaire de la marque Miss Sixty. L'architecture et le design reflètent la quête d'innovation en misant sur les dernières tendances. Les touches d'un style classique revisité sont mises en valeur dans le hall dont les murs sont recouverts de mosaïques aux motifs baroques dans un doré tout en élégance. Les lignes épurées des comptoir et bar se mêlent à ce revêtement et à certains détails, à l'instar du lustre moderne et de la photographie qui occupe tout le mur latéral, au-dessus des divans du lobby. Une élégance moderne définit l'entrée de cet hôtel, reflet de l'esprit audacieux de la mode juvénile.

Il Sixty Hotel è la prima incursione nel settore alberghiero effettuata dal proprietario del noto marchio di moda Miss Sixty. L'architettura e il design di questo hotel riflettono la ricerca dell'innovazione e la scommessa sulle ultime tendenze. Le pennellate di uno stile classico rivisitato si fanno evidenti nella hall, le cui pareti sono rivestite da un mosaico con motivi barocchi in eleganti tonalità dorate. Le linee sobrie del banco della reception si mescolano con questo rivestimento e con particolari come il moderno chandelier o la fotografia che occupa tutta la parete laterale, posta sui divani della lobby. Una raffinatezza dai toni moderni caratterizza l'ingresso di questo albergo, specchio dello spirito disinibito ed audace della moda giovanile.

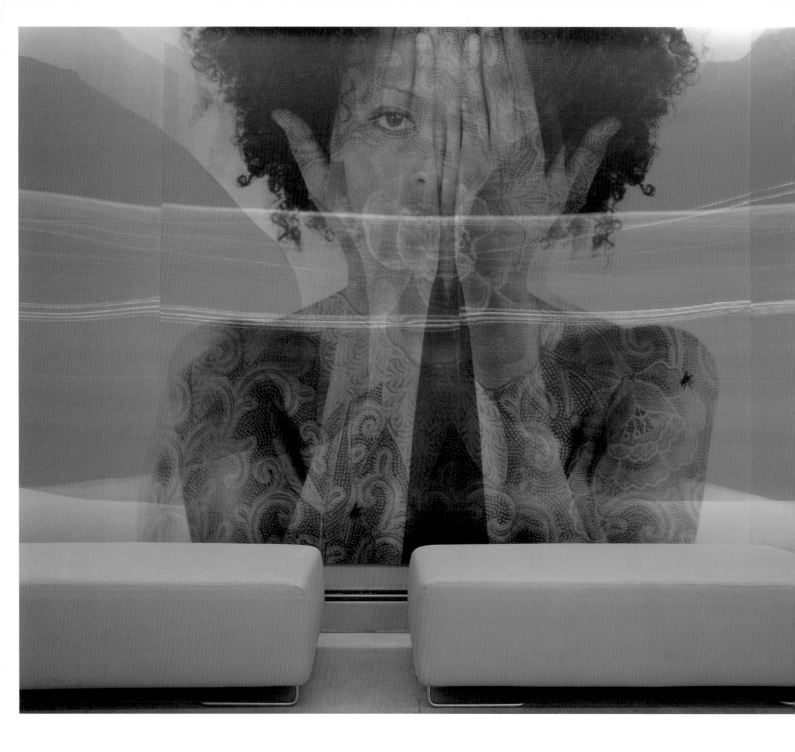

TOMÁS ALÍA | MADRID, SPAIN

Website	www.tomasalia.com
Project	Nueva Fontana
Location	Madrid, Spain
Year of completion	2005
Photo credits	Estudio Tomás Alía

Nueva Fontana's space hides behind a black granite façade and includes a club and a restaurant whose aesthetic is clearly a homage to artists from the 40s, like Alfred Porteneuve or André Arbus. Standing out in the Nueva Fontana club is the long walkway and the large shell-shaped stage molded in steel. A retro lighting system is present throughout the space, which allows for changes in color. The oval bar has been surfaced in black and white Bisazza mosaic, beneath glass Swarovsky lights. The Azabara restaurant transmits sobriety and elegance. Its design includes both the black and white mosaic floor and late art deco furniture.

Hinter der Fassade aus schwarzem Granit verbirgt sich das Nueva Fontana, ein Club und ein Restaurant, deren Gestaltung Designern der Vierzigerjahre wie Alfred Porteneuve und André Arbus alle Ehren erweist. Der Club Nueva Fontana wird von einem langen Laufsteg und einer großen, muschelförmigen Bühne aus Stahl beherrscht. Durch ein Retrobeleuchtungssystem ist ein Farbwechsel möglich. Die ovale Bar ist mit schwarz-weißem Bisazzamosaik verkleidet und mit Lampen aus Swaroskikristall ausgestattet. Das schlichte und elegante Restaurant Azabara ist mit einem schwarz-weißen Mosaikboden und Möbeln im Stil eines späten Art déco dekoriert.

Tras la fachada de granito negro se esconde el espacio Nueva Fontana, que incluye un club y un restaurante cuya estética es un claro homenaje a autores de los años 40, como Alfred Porteneuve o André Arbus. En el club Nueva Fontana llama la atención la larga pasarela y el gran escenario con forma de concha modulada en acero. Todo el conjunto dispone de un sistema de retroiluminación que le permite cambiar de color. La barra ovalada está realizada en mosaico de Bisazza en blanco y negro, bajo lámparas de cristal de Swarovsky. En el restaurante Azabara destacan la sobriedad y la elegancia, cuyo diseño apuesta tanto por el mosaico en blanco y negro del suelo como por el mobiliario art déco tardío.

Derrière la façade en granit noir, se cache l'espace Nueva Fontana, qui comprend un club et un restaurant dont l'esthétique est un hommage incontestable aux auteurs des années 40, comme Alfred Porteneuve ou André Arbus. Dans le club Nueva Fontana, le regard est attiré par la longue passerelle et la grande scène en forme de coquillage, moulée dans l'acier. Tout l'ensemble dispose d'un système d'éclairage réversible permettant de moduler la couleur. Le bar ovale est réalisé en mosaïque de Bisazza noire et blanche, éclairé par des lampes en cristal de Swarovsky. La sobriété et l'élégance ressortent dans le restaurant Azabara, dont le design mise autant sur la mosaïque noire et blanche du sol que sur le mobilier Art Déco tardif.

Dietro la facciata di granito nero si nasconde lo spazio Nueva Fontana, che include un club e un ristorante la cui estetica è un chiaro omaggio ad autori degli anni 40 come Alfred Porteneuve o André Arbus. Nel club Nueva Fontana ad attirare l'attenzione è la lunga passerella e il grande scenario a forma di conchiglia modulata in acciaio. Tutto l'insieme dispone di un sistema di retroilluminazione che gli permette di cambiare colore. Il banco dalla forma ovale, realizzato in mosaico di Bisazza bianco e nero, giace sotto lampade di cristallo di Swarovsky. Nel ristorante Azabara spiccano la sobrietà e l'eleganza, espresse mediante un mosaico in bianco e nero per il pavimento e un arredamento in stile tarda art déco.

TOMÁS ALÍA | MADRID, SPAIN

Website	www.tomasalia.com
Project	Sol y Sombra
Location	Madrid, Spain
Year of completio	2006
Photo credits	Luis Hevia

Stereotypes from the world of bull fighting and flamenco have been reinvented at the hands of designer Tomás Alía. This space has a modern, avant-garde aesthetic based on Spanish traditions. The most unequivocal symbols have been transformed into decorative elements, as is the case with the large comb that has been converted here in to the bar, or the jackets of the bullfighters, that shine on the large mural across the wall. This original result is achieved through the combination of ethnic and traditional objects with avant-garde materials and modern items of furniture. The lighting system, based on LEDs, bathes the space in different colors affording a touch of chic, and a contrast to this purely traditional inspiration.

Die Klischees aus der Welt des Stierkampfes und des Flamencos wurden von dem Designer Tomás Alía neu erfunden. Es handelt sich um ein Lokal mit einer modernen, avantgardistischen Ästhetik, die auf den spanischen Traditionen basiert. Die eindeutigsten Symbole wurden in Dekorationselemente verwandelt, so der große Zierkamm, der zur Bar wurde, und die Jacken der Stierkämpfer, die ein großes Wandgemälde bilden. Dieses originelle Ergebnis erreichte man durch die Verbindung volkstümlicher und traditioneller Objekte mit avantgardistischen Materialien und modernen Möbeln. Die LED-Beleuchtung taucht das Lokal in unterschiedliche Farben, ein schicker Gegensatz zu den rein traditionell inspirierten Elementen.

Los tópicos del mundo taurino y del flamenco han sido reinventados de la mano del diseñador Tomás Alía. Se trata de un local con estética moderna y vanguardista basada en tradiciones españolas. Los símbolos más inequívocos han sido transformados en elementos decorativos, como es el caso de la gran peineta que se convierte aquí en una barra de bar, o las chaquetas de los toreros, que resplandecen en el gran mural a lo largo de la pared. Este original resultado se consigue con la mezcla de objetos étnicos y tradicionales junto con materiales vanguardistas y piezas de mobiliario moderno. La tecnología lumínica basada en los LEDS que bañan el local en distintos colores contrasta con esta inspiración puramente tradicional, aportando un aire *chic*.

Les éléments de l'univers taurin et du flamenco ont été réinventés par le talent du designer Tomás Alía. Il s'agit d'un établissement à l'esthétique moderne et avant-gardiste basée sur les traditions espagnoles. Les symboles les plus évidents sont transformés en éléments décoratifs, à l'instar du grand peigne de mantille qui se métamorphose ici en comptoir de bar, ou encore les vestes des toreros qui resplendissent sur la grande peinture murale le long du mur. L'originalité résulte du mélange d'objets ethniques et traditionnels à côté de matériaux avant-gardistes et de pièces de mobilier moderne. La technologie d'éclairage basée sur les LEDs, qui baignent l'établissement dans diverses couleurs, contraste avec l'inspiration purement traditionnelle, conférant à l'ensemble un air *chic*.

I luoghi comuni del mondo taurino e del flamenco sono stati reinventati per mano del disegnatore Tomàs Alía. Si tratta di un locale dall'estetica moderna e all'avanguardia basata sulle tipiche tradizioni spagnole. I simboli più inequivocabili sono stati trasformati in elementi decorativi, come è il caso del grande pettine che qui diventa il banco di un bar, o le giacche dei toreri, i cui ricami brillano nel grande murale lungo tutta la parete. Per ottenere questo singolare risultato, si sono mescolati oggetti etnici e tradizionali con materiali di ultima generazione e pezzi di mobilia moderna. L'illuminazione, basata sui LED che bagnano il locale in diversi colori, è in contrasto con questa ispirazione puramente tradizionale, e apporta una certa atmosfera chic.

YOO / PHILIPPE STARCK | LONDON, UNITED KINGDOM

Website	www.yooarehere.com
	www.philippe-starck.com
Project	Yoo Copenhagen
Location	Copenhagen, Denmark
Year of completion	2006
Photo credits	Yoo

It is quite impossible to ignore the Phillipe Starck hallmark in this apartment. And logically so, given that he led the team of Yoo professionals, whose services are offered to those with a hectic lifestyle and no time to decorate and furnish their home. They are much more than a simple interior design studio and they offer three different packages which include complete furniture and accessories, from the very basic to more elaborate concepts. The result is striking: an eclectic blend of styles enhanced by classic pieces which have been modernised in a luxurious ambience with great charcter.

Der Einfluss von Philippe Starck in der Gestaltung dieser Wohnung ist unverkennbar. Das ist logisch, denn der Designer leitet das Team von Yoo, das Personen, denen die Hektik des Alltags keine Zeit dazu lässt, ihre Wohnung möbliert und dekoriert. Es handelt sich nicht um ein einfaches Studio für Raumgestaltung: Es bietet den Kunden drei verschiedene Pakete an, die Möbel und Zubehör einschließen, von einem Basispaket bis zu einem Komplettpaket. Das Ergebnis ist auffallend – eine eklektische Stilmischung aus klassischen, modernisierten Möbeln in einer sehr persönlichen, luxuriösen Wohnumgebung.

Es imposible pasar por alto la influencia del estilo de Philippe Starck en este apartamento. Y es lógico, pues el diseñador encabeza el equipo de profesionales de Yoo, cuyos servicios se ofrecen a aquellas personas cuya vida ajetreada les priva de tiempo para amueblar y decorar su vivienda. No son un simple estudio de interiorismo y su oferta permite a sus clientes escoger entre tres *packs* distintos que incluyen mobiliario y complementos, desde el más básico hasta el más completo. El resultado salta a la vista: una mezcla ecléctica de estilos encabezada por muebles clásicos modernizados en un conjunto que desprende lujo con mucha personalidad.

Dans cet appartement, on ne peut ignorer l'influence du style de Philippe Starck. Et c'est normal, car le designer dirige l'équipe de professionnels du Yoo qui offre ses services à ces personnes dont la vie agitée ne leur laisse pas le temps de meubler et décorer leur habitation. Le designer ne fait pas une simple étude d'aménagement intérieur, mais propose à ses clients de choisir entre trois formules distinctes qui comprennent mobilier et accessoires, du plus basique au plus complet. Le résultat est éblouissant : un mélange éclectique de styles avec en tête des meubles classiques modernisés dans un ensemble qui dégage un luxe très caractérisé.

È quasi impossibile non notare l'influenza dello stile di Philippe Stark in questo appartamento. Non a caso infatti l'enfant terrible del design moderno è il direttore creativo di Yoo, l'innovativa società di progettazione che strizza l'occhio al compratore sensibile al design ma con poco tempo per arredare la propria abitazione. Non si tratta comunque di un semplice studio di interior design. La Yoo permette ai suoi clienti di scegliere tra tre pack diversi che includono mobilia e accessori, da quelli di base ai più completi. Il risultato è più che evidente: una mescolanza eclettica di stili dove predominano i mobili classici accuratamente modernizzati e immersi in un insieme che sprizza lusso e personalità.

INDEX

© 2008 daab
cologne london new york

published and distributed worldwide by
daab gmbh
friesenstr. 50
d-50670 köln

p +49 - 221 - 913 927 0
f +49 - 221 - 913 927 20

mail@daab-online.com
www.daab-online.com

publisher ralf daab
rdaab@daab-online.com

creative director feyyaz
mail@feyyaz.com

editorial project by loft publications
© 2008 loft publications

editor and texts aitana lleonart

layout conxi papió
english translation jay noden, heather baggot
german translation susanne engler
french translation marion westerhoff
italian translation maurizio siliato

front cover "suite milan" by bisazza © federico cedrone, ottavio tomasini

back cover ciolino house © anson smart

printed in china
www.everbest.eu

isbn 978-3-86654-017-0